Rumi and Islam

Selections from His Stories, Poems, and Discourses

Other books in the
SkyLight Illuminations Series

Rumi and Islam

Selections from His Stories, Poems, and Discourses

Annotated & Explained

Translation & Annotation
by Ibrahim Gamard

Walking Together, Finding the Way
SKYLIGHT PATHS Publishing
Woodstock, Vermont

Rumi and Islam: Selections from His Stories, Poems, and Discourses
Annotated & Explained

First Printing 2004
Translation, annotation, and introductory material © 2004 by Ibrahim Gamard

Library of Congress Cataloging-in-Publication Data

Jalāl al-Dīn Rūmī, Maulana, 1207–1273.
[Selections. English. 2004]
Rumi and Islam: selections from his stories, poems, and discourses annotated & explained / translation & annotation by Ibrahim Gamard.
p. cm.—(SkyLight Illuminations)
Includes bibliographical references (p.   ) and index.
ISBN 1-59473-002-4
1. Jalāl al-Dīn Rūmī, Maulana, 1207–1273—Religion. 2. Mevleviyeh. 3. Sufism.
I. Gamard, Ibrahim. II. Title. III. Series.
BP189.7.M4 J3513 2004
297.4—dc22

2003026380

10 9 8 7 6 5 4 3 2 1

Manufactured in the United States of America

SkyLight Paths Publishing is creating a place where people of different spiritual traditions come together for challenge and inspiration, a place where we can help each other understand the mystery that lies at the heart of our existence.

SkyLight Paths sees both believers and seekers as a community that increasingly transcends traditional boundaries of religion and denomination—people wanting to learn from each other, *walking together, finding the way*.

Walking Together, Finding the Way
Published by SkyLight Paths Publishing
A Division of LongHill Partners, Inc.
Sunset Farm Offices, Route 4, P.O. Box 237
Woodstock, VT 05091
Tel: (802) 457-4000   Fax: (802) 457-4004
www.skylightpaths.com

I would like to dedicate this book to Shaykh Shafīq Jān of Istanbul, the chief spiritual director *(Sar-i Tarīqat)* of the Mevlevi (Whirling Dervishes) order of Islamic Sufism, who, now in his mid-nineties, has been studying the works of Rumi in Persian since boyhood, who has written books that translate and explain Rumi's poetry and teachings in the Turkish language, and who comes from a long lineage of Mevlevi scholars able to understand and appreciate Rumi's words and teachings in the original Persian.

I also dedicate this book to lovers of Rumi's poetry everywhere who are interested in attaining a deeper understanding of his sublime spiritual wisdom.

Contents ☐

Praises of the Prophet

Preface □

I first began studying the *Mathnawi*, Jalaluddin Rumi's poetic masterpiece of Islamic mystical wisdom, in 1975. My wife, Sher, and I were living in Los Angeles, California, in a center for Sufi studies. Every Thursday night we whirled with several others in Turkish dervish costumes, and our teacher, Reshad Feild, gave a lecture to guests and led Sufi chanting. One day, he told us that the head of the Mevlevi (Whirling Dervishes) Sufi order in Turkey was coming to America for the first time in order to visit us. He was Suleyman Loras Dede, from Konya, the very city where Rumi lived and is buried. Dede was the chief spiritual leader [*shaykh*] of the Mevlevi Sufi order, which has maintained the spiritual teachings and practices of Rumi and his successors for more than seven hundred years.

In preparation for Dede's upcoming visit, I spent several months reading the *Mathnawi* in R. A. Nicholson's complete translation—over fourteen hundred pages of dense, antiquated-sounding, and highly academic British English. In this book I found many passages that were exquisitely and rapturously mystical, full of the mystic lover's ecstatic love for God (described as the Only Beloved and Friend) and God's Infinite Love and Mercy in response. I found this book to be the greatest work of religious mysticism that I had ever found in all my explorations of mysticism in world traditions (a conviction I continue to hold).

When Suleyman Dede arrived in Los Angeles in 1976, he blessed our tall conical hats, taught us the basics of the famous Mevlevi "Whirling Prayer Ceremony," and led the ceremony in full costumes in a local gymnasium—a ritual of great spiritual blessings (and one in which my wife and I continue to participate). The next year my wife and I visited him in Turkey, where we visited Rumi's tomb, a place full of the "perfume" of God's Love. I asked a

Western woman who translated for Dede's English-speaking disciples there whether we could learn what Dede had to teach about the *Mathnawi*. She replied that this would be far too difficult to translate from Turkish.

About five years later, I decided to teach myself Persian in order to study the *Mathnawi* in its original text. I bought a small introductory grammar and soon learned to find words in a large Persian-English dictionary. I then looked up every word in the first couplet of the *Mathnawi:* "Listen to the reed-flute, how it complains of separations." During the next years, I gradually read the entire text in Persian, with the help of Nicholson's literal translation.

In 1985, I heard that there was a new professor of Persian literature, an Afghan, at the University of California, Berkeley. After I met Dr. Ravan Farhadi, he proposed that we translate all of the nearly two thousand quatrains attributed to Rumi. We have worked on this project in our spare time ever since (it is now an unpublished manuscript, "The Quatrains of Rumi"). Over the years, Dr. Farhadi's correction of my translation efforts has been an invaluable help in learning the Persian of Rumi's time, and this, together with accurate published translations, has given me the good fortune of learning to appreciate and understand Rumi's mystical poetry and spiritual teachings.

In 1997 I began posting articles on the Internet about translation issues, such as the lack of accuracy in popular versions of Rumi's poetry. The next year I was invited to add explanatory footnotes and transliterations of the Persian words to selections of Nicholson's translations of the *Mathnawi* on a Rumi Listserv group called "Sunlight." During the following year I was invited to submit my own translations for the members of the group. For the next couple of years I translated one selection per week, together with transliterations from the Persian text and explanatory footnotes. For the footnotes, I used Nicholson's two volumes of commentary on the *Mathnawi*, later supplemented by a Persian translation of the well-known seventeenth-century Ottoman Turkish commentary by the Mevlevi scholar Anqaravi.

By the end of 2001, after having made quite a few translations of selections from the *Mathnawi*, I decided to create my own *Mathnawi* website and post all the translations for anyone who was interested. I hoped that some of the lovers of Rumi's poetry would be motivated to go beyond the popular versions and study in depth the meanings of Rumi's words and spiritual teachings, verse by verse, in short selections.

And as a Muslim (since 1984), I was also interested in explaining Rumi's frequent Islamic references (to beliefs, verses from the Qur'an, sayings of the Prophet Muhammad, and so on) that permeate his vast outpouring of poetry. I wanted to convey Rumi's love and veneration for the profound wisdom contained in the verses of the Holy Qur'an and the sayings of the Prophet.

I was delighted when an editor from SkyLight Paths Publishing contacted me, after seeing my Rumi translations and commentary on my website, and proposed a book of translations and explanations of Rumi's stories about the Prophet Muhammad—in essentially the same format I had been using.

This book you are now holding is a selection of what I believe are the best of Rumi's accounts of the compassionate actions, sayings, and qualities of the Prophet, which include Rumi's own inspired comments and explanations. It is my hope that you will be surprised and uplifted by the profound wisdom that Jalaluddin Rumi conveys through these stories and sayings of the Prophet.

I also hope that it will educate Western lovers of Rumi's poetry about the Islamic foundations of his lover-Beloved mystical poetry. And I hope that it will also educate Muslim readers, who may be skeptical of Islamic mysticism (Sufism) and the poetry of Rumi, about how Mawlana Jalaluddin Rumi was one of the greatest Muslim followers of the Prophet Muhammad, and how his Jesus-like teachings about the nature of love for God and God's Love for us are most suitable for increasing the appreciation of Islamic wisdom in the West.

Introduction ☐

Mawlana Jalaluddin Rumi (may God sanctify his spirit) was one of the greatest Muslim saints and mystics. He has been hailed by one Western scholar as "surely the greatest mystical poet in the history of mankind."[1] It is extraordinary how popularized versions of his poetry have made his name so well known in America and Europe in recent years—after more than seven hundred years, during which his fame has endured in the Middle East, Central Asia, and the Indian subcontinent.

The popularity of his poetry has spread in the West because of its heartfelt themes of lover-Beloved mysticism and its spiritual joy, which emanate even from the most distorted versions in English. This popularization, however, has entailed several sacrifices: a lack of accuracy of the meanings of his words and teachings, and a deliberate minimization and omission of verses that express his profound Muslim piety as a dedicated follower of the prayerful daily life exemplified by the Prophet Muhammad (may God pour blessings upon him).

This popularization has been so successful that many people think of Rumi as someone who started out as a Muslim and a dry scholar and then became transformed into a universal mystic who transcended any particular religion. This false impression is also the result of frequently quoted verses that have been attributed to Rumi but are not authentic, such as these:

> O Muslims, what advice *do you have?*—since I don't know myself: I'm neither Christian nor Jew; I'm neither Zoroastrian nor Muslim.[2]

> I traversed *the lands of* the Cross and the Christians, *but* he wasn't in the Cross. I traveled to the temple of idols, to the ancient temple,

but there wasn't even a tinge evident within it.... I pulled the reins
of seeking toward the Ka'ba, *but* He wasn't in that destination of old
and young.... I looked into my own heart *and* I saw Him in that place;
He wasn't in any *other* place.[3]

Return *in repentance,* return! Whatever you are, return!
    Even if you are an unbeliever or a Zoroastrian *fire worshipper* or
an idol worshipper, return!
    This *Sufi* court of ours is not a court of despair.
    Even if you have broken your repentance a hundred times,
return![4]

These are genuine Persian Sufi verses, but were not composed by Rumi.

Some authentic verses have been interpreted as more universal than
they are. For example, in one story Rumi represented God as saying to the
Prophet Moses, who had criticized the heartfelt prayer of a simple shepherd:

The idiomatic speech of *the country of* Hind is the *mode of* praise *of
God* for the Hindians, *and* the idiomatic speech of Sind is the *mode
of* praise *of God* for the Sindians. I do not become pure and holy by
their praise, but they become purified and shining *by it.* We do not
regard the tongue and *outward* speech, *but* We regard the soul and
the *inward* state.[5]

Here, Rumi chose the terms *Hinduwān* and *Sindiyān* for the sake of
the rhyme—not out of acceptance of the Hindu religion, which he would
have viewed as involving polytheism and idolatry. Instead, he was referring—for the sake of his Muslim listeners—to Indian Muslims who spoke
the language of the people in the countries along the Indus River.[6] The
meaning here is that the spiritual quality and intention of the prayers of
worshipers of One God are more important than the outward form of
expression, such as the language used.

    Another example of an authentic quote is this: "The creed of Love
of God is distinct from all religions; the creed and doctrine of the lovers is
God *alone."*[7] Rumi taught that the essence of worship is constant devotion and love for God alone. He called this "the creed of Love," "the creed

of the lovers," and "the school of Love." However, he did not intend "the creed of Love" to mean a religion or sect separate from Islam, but the pure essence of the worship of God, of a different quality than the externals of Islamic worship. He said, "What is the ascension to Heaven? *It is this being 'nothing.'* For the lovers *of God,* the creed and religion is being annihilated of self."[8]

Despite popular beliefs about Rumi, there is actually little evidence that he knew much about other religions, other than what he learned from a traditional Islamic education. Rumi had occasional contacts with Christians and learned some of the local Anatolian Greek dialect.[9] During one conversation in Arabic, he denied the assertion of a Christian that Jesus is God [Allāh] and gave a strong response: "How could it be allowed *as a possibility* that a trail person...*with* a body shorter than two cubits could be the keeper and preserver of the seven heavens...?"[10] This was in accord with the Qur'an's denial of the divinity of Jesus (5:19), as well as with a verse which addresses the "People of the Book" (Jews and Christians): "We do not worship *anyone* except God and we do not associate any as a partner with Him" (3:64). On another occasion Rumi compared the way of Christian monks (renouncing the world, not marrying, living in isolation and in mountains) to the way of the Prophet (living in the world, marrying, enduring the injustices of men and women, struggling against one's own pride and jealousy, and thereby correcting one's character). Then he said, "If you are unable to travel the path of Muhammad, at least travel the path of Jesus, so that you may not remain entirely excluded."[11] Here, Rumi was consistent with the verse which states that Christians are "closest in affection" to the believers (in the Islamic revelation), "since among them are priests and monks who are not arrogant" (Qur'an 5:85). On another occasion, when a Greek mason was building a fireplace for Rumi's house, his companions said to the man in a jesting manner, "Why don't you become a Muslim, since the best of religions is the religion of Islam?" The mason replied that he had been involved in the religion of Jesus for close to fifty years, that he was in (pious) fear of him and would be ashamed to forsake his religion. Rumi suddenly came in through the doorway and spoke, making a pun in Persian: "The secret of faith is fear [tars], so anyone who is afraid [tarsā] of God, even if he is a Christian [Tarsā], he possesses religion and is not lacking religion." And then Rumi left.[12] In this situation, his response was in accord with the verse "Among the People of the Book are some who... hurry to do good deeds, and they are among the righteous. And whatever good *deeds* they do *the reward for them* will not be denied. And God knows those who are piously fearing *of Him*" (Qur'an 3:113–115). In a similar story, when a drunk barged into an ecstatic spiritual gathering and bumped against Rumi, his companions began to beat him. Rumi criticized them for acting like bad drunkards, while it was the man who had drunk wine. They said that the man was a Christian, and Rumi replied, "He is a Christian [Tarsā], *but* why are you not afraid [tarsā] *of the judgment of God*?"[13]

Rumi had cordial relations with Christians in the town of Konya, especially monks and priests. He went occasionally to the St. Amphilochius church that, according to an Arab legend, contained the tomb of Plato. As a result, Muslims, some of whom believed that Plato was a Prophet, visited the site, which they called "Plato's Monastery."[14] Rumi is said to have stayed there on retreat a number of times,[15] doing prodigious acts of asceticism that impressed the monks so much that at least one of them was said to have become his disciple. This friendly relationship continued after Rumi's death, and his grandson, Ūlū 'Ārif Chelebī, is reported to have participated with his disciples in a three-day feast at the church.[16] Such was the reverence for Rumi's saintliness in Konya that Christians and Jews flocked to his funeral procession and could not be prevented from joining it.[17]

The Muslim regent who ruled Konya was married to a Christian princess known as the "Georgian Lady," who was said to be a disciple and supporter of Rumi. It is related that one day she asked the architect who built the green domed shrine over Rumi's tomb what miracle of Rumi's led him to become so captivated by him that he became his disciple and held such immense love for him. He said, "The least of our Master's miracles is this: while, in the case of every Prophet, there is a nation who love him; and in the case of every Sufi master [*shaykh*], there is a people who have become his imitating followers—*people of* all nations and rulers of dominions are in complete accord in having love for our venerable Master, have been honored by listening to his [*exposition of spiritual*] secrets, and are enthusiastically boasting [*about having met him*]. What miracle could be more great than this?"[18]

Through the path of mystical Islam and the blessings of God, Rumi had many experiences of transcendent oneness, which he sometimes described in poetic speeches by people in his stories. An example is a verse describing an ecstatic state of consciousness in the story of Zayd, who is represented as saying, "From that *transcendent* viewpoint, all religions are one, and a hundred thousand years and a single hour are one."[19] This verse also should not be interpreted to mean that Rumi was expressing approval for other religions or saying that religious differences don't matter. Rather, it expresses a sublime mystical awareness beyond the ordinary human mind in which all separateness has vanished (see note 2 corresponding to chapter 12, "Zayd"). It also accords with how some mystics of Islam have interpreted the verse "There is no divinity except *the One True* God" (Qur'an 47:19) to mean that, in the absolute sense, idolators and polytheists in their ignorance are still worshiping the One True God, since ultimately there exists no other. The same may be said about the verse "Whichever way you turn, there is the Face of God" (2:115), which may have been the inspiration for a number of Islamic Sufi spiritual practices, such as whirling prayer movements.

If you are thinking that the "Muslim Rumi" described here is not the Rumi that you have come to revere and love, the "Rumi of Universal Love"—that Rumi who was filled with pure love for God and for all of creation—was real; his soul remains in sanctified nearness to God, and the blessing of his spirit lives through his poetry and words and at his tomb in Turkey. You can read in other books about Rumi's use of Persian mystical metaphors—about the reed-flute's shrill cry of longing for its original home in the reed field, the nightingale's passionate love songs for the rose, the self-sacrificing love of the moth for the candle flame, the yearning of the water for the thirsty man, and so on. You may have read descriptions and poems about Rumi's extraordinary mystical love for his Sufi master and friend, Shams-i Tabrīzī. But now read about his reverence and love for the Prophet Muhammad. With this book you are invited to let go, for a time, of whatever attachment you may have to the popularized image of Rumi you have read or heard about, and to allow Rumi to be the Muslim he was. Read here a very different selection of Rumi translations than you have encountered before. Hopefully, the annotations will help you understand and appreciate them more clearly, and drink cup after cup of his extraordinary God-given supply of sublime spiritual wisdom.

About Rumi

Rumi was born in the year 1207 C.E. in what is now the nation of Tājikistān (the country north of Afghanistan) in a valley known as Wakhsh, where his father worked as a Muslim preacher and scholar. This was part of the cultural area of the ancient city of Balkh (in present-day Afghanistan), which had been a major center of Islamic learning for five hundred years before Rumi was born. His father, also a great mystic, or Sufi master, was from Balkh. He named his son Muhammad but later called him by the additional name Jalālu 'd-dīn ("the Glory of the Faith"). His full name was Jalālu 'd-dīn Muhammad bin (= son of) Husayn al-Balkhī. Later, when he moved to Anatolia (present-day Turkey) with his family, he became known as Jalālu 'd-dīn Muhammad al-Rūmī.

The reason for this was that the Anatolian peninsula for centuries had been called Rūm (a form of "Rome"), which meant "the Greek-occupied lands" (Greeks had long ruled the area from Constantinople, the capital of the Eastern Roman Empire and later of the Byzantine Empire). Rumi has always been known in the East by the respectful title of Mawlānā, which means "our Master" in Arabic. He is known as Mawlānā-yi Rūm in India and Pakistan, Mawlānā Jalālu'd-dīn-i Balkhī in Afghanistan,

Mevlana in Turkey, and Mōlavī in Iran. Only in the West has he been known by the less respectful and less accurate name Rumi ("the Greek").

Rumi must have memorized much or all of the Holy Qur'an when he was young, because the *Mathnawi* and his other poetry are filled with direct quotes in Arabic, Persian paraphrases, and references to Qur'anic verses. He belonged to the Hanafī school of Islamic law, one of the four orthodox legal traditions of the Sunnī branch of Islam. This means that his daily religious behavior was faithful to the many details of the Hanafī tradition of how to follow the example of the Prophet Muhammad.

Rumi's first Sufi master, Sayyid Burhānu 'd-dīn Termezī, was his father's leading Sufi disciple who came to Anatolia after hearing of the death of Rumi's father. Rumi was his Sufi disciple for nine years, during part of which he was sent to Syria to obtain a traditional Islamic education. Sayyid Burhānu 'd-dīn was also a profound mystic who instilled in Rumi a love of Persian Sufi poetry and ordered him to do a number of lengthy solitary prayer retreats.

Rumi was thirty-seven years old when he met his second Sufi master, Shamsu 'd-dīn (the "Sun of the Religion") Muhammad al-Tabrīzī (also spelled in Persian form as Shams-i Tabrīzī), who was originally from the Persian city of Tabrīz. Shams traditionally was believed to have been about sixty years old at the time. It is now known that Shams was not an illiterate and "wild" dervish, as previously thought by Western scholars. He had a solid Islamic education and was literate and fluent in Arabic as well as in Persian. And Shams himself belonged to another major orthodox school of Sunnī Islamic law, called Shāfi'ī. In the "Discourses of Shams," a collection of notes recorded by his disciples (among whom was Rumi's son, Sultān Walad), Shams reveals himself to have been not only a profound mystic but very knowledgeable about traditional and mystical interpretations of verses from the Qur'an and sayings of the Prophet Muhammad. And he criticized at least one famous Sufi master for not following the daily religious behavior of the Prophet.[20]

A hagiography of Rumi written by a disciple of Rumi's grandson, Aflākī, contains many miracle stories as well as accounts of how Rumi prayed the five daily ritual Islamic prayers, fasted during the month of Ramadān, and did many extended voluntary fasts. In numerous accounts he voiced traditional Islamic beliefs on many topics. This biography states that when one of Rumi's closest disciples offered to stop following his own (Shāfi'ī) school of Islamic law and to follow Rumi's (Hanafī) school instead, Rumi said, "No! no! The right *thing to do* is this: that you should be in your own school of *Islamic* law and maintain it, but you should travel in my *Islamic mystical* Way and provide right guidance to people about my path of Love."[21]

But it is the masterpiece of his later life, the *Mathnawi,* in which he reveals himself as both a profound mystic and an extremely devout Muslim. And a study of his stories and sayings of the Prophet Muhammad reveals his veneration and love for the Holy Prophet and the Revelation of the Qur'an.

Mawlana Jalaluddin Muhammad Rumi died in 1273 and was buried next to his father's tomb in Konya, Turkey. The anniversary of his death was commemorated for centuries according to the Islamic lunar calendar, but it has been celebrated in Turkey for the past fifty years according to the Western solar calendar on December 17. On that night, Mevlevis all over the world whirl in remembrance and for the glorification of God, and many different kinds of groups read Rumi's poetry in their own languages.

About Rumi's Works

Rumi began composing poetry at about the age of thirty-seven as a result of the spiritual turbulence he experienced after meeting his second Sufi teacher, Shams-i Tabrīzī. He wrote more than five thousand poems (mostly odes and quatrains), which make up his *Dīvān,* or collected works of poetry. The *Dīvān* is filled with ecstatic verses in which Rumi expresses his mystical love for Shams-i Tabrīzī as a symbol of his love for God. He was overjoyed at being with his spiritual master and was devastated by their separation. Shams disappeared twice, the first time when his life was threatened by some of Rumi's disciples and the people of Konya, who were jealous because of their lack of contact with Rumi. After the two had closely associated for about a year and a half, Shams left. He was found to be in Syria. He returned—accompanied by Rumi's son, whom Rumi had sent to invite Shams back—about six months later. After another six months, Shams married a young woman who had been brought up in Rumi's household. However, she became ill and died shortly afterward, and Shams soon disappeared permanently.

About fifteen years later, after a period of further spiritual transformation resulting from meeting and losing such an extraordinary spiritual teacher, Rumi was asked by one of his disciples to compose a lengthy poem called a *mathnawī*, consisting of rhymed couplets. Rumi's disciples had been studying similar works composed by two earlier Persian Sufi poets (Sanā'ī and 'Attār), and the request was for Rumi to present his spiritual teachings in a similar form, so as to be pleasing to recite and easy to memorize. Rumi spent the last fifteen years of his life dictating this type of poetry to his favorite disciple. Rumi's *Mathnawī-yi Ma'nawī* ("Rhymed Couplets of Deep Spiritual Meaning") is a collection of Sufi stories, ethical teachings, and mystical teachings. It is filled with Qur'anic meanings and references. Rumi himself called the *Mathnawi* "the roots of the roots of the roots of the (Islamic) Religion…and the explainer of the Qur'an."[22] It consists of six books, totaling more than twenty-five thousand couplets.

In addition, there are collections of Rumi's words in prose: his *Discourses* and *Sermons* (based on notes of his talks and lectures written down by his disciples), as well as his *Letters*. All of these have frequent quotes from the Qur'an, references to the Prophet Muhammad, and prayers in Arabic.

About the Prophet Muhammad

Muhammad was born in the year 570 C.E. in Mecca, a major commercial town in Arabia. The prosperity of the town was due to its location on a major trade route as well as being the site of a well-known shrine, the Ka'ba, which contained 360 idols. Muhammad must have felt an affinity with the views of Arabs called *Hunafā*, of whom he had heard. These individuals were deeply ashamed of Arab polytheistic worship but were not attracted to Judaism or Christianity. They wanted, instead, to practice as best they could the pure monotheism of the Prophet Abraham, the ancestor of the Arab people.

When the Revelation of the Qur'an was given to Muhammad and he became a Prophet (in the same line as the Prophets Abraham, Moses, and Jesus), he was forty years old. He was so shocked and bewildered that he went immediately to his wife of fifteen years, Khadīja, for comfort and advice. She was the first to accept that he had indeed been chosen by God as a true Prophet and Messenger. Khadīja had been a wealthy widow and had employed Muhammad to be in charge of her caravans until they eventually married. He remained monogamous for another ten years until her death, after which he had multiple wives (mostly widows, some of whom he married in order to increase unity among the Arab tribes).

The Prophet and his growing number of followers who joined the renewal of the Abrahamic Revelation had been cruelly persecuted by the great majority of polytheists in Mecca during the early years, and there were plots against the Prophet's life, until he received a revelation that he should flee to another town, later named Medina, where a group of Muslims had invited him to live. This event, in the year 622, was the famous "Migration" [*Hijrah*] and marks the beginning of the Muslim calendar. Threatened by alliances of pagan Arab tribes who planned to advance on Medina in order to exterminate the new monotheists, the Prophet received a revelation a year later that authorized fighting the attackers—after he and his followers had endured persecution nonviolently for thirteen years.

The many inspiring accounts of the Prophet's behavior in various situations reveal him as a person of extraordinary compassion and wisdom. But he often lived an ordinary life when at home in Medina: sweeping, sewing, and mending his own clothes and sandals; tending to the animals; and going to the market. He visited anyone who he heard was sick, joined in any funeral procession he saw, and accepted dinner invitations from slaves. There were many years of harsh poverty, during which there was little for him and his family to eat—sometimes nothing more than the "two blacks": dates and muddy water.

The Prophet Muhammad died in the year 632 C.E., and was buried in his house in Medina, a site adjoining his mosque (also a site of an extraordinary presence of holiness), now encompassed by a massive complex to shade many thousands of worshipers.

The accounts of the Prophet's actions and sayings are called Traditions (Ahādīth, singular: Hadīth). Next to the Holy Qur'an itself, these are the next level of authority for the implementation of Islam.

The mystics of Islam (also called Sufis, dervishes, and faqīrs) maintain the practice of Islam as their foundation (including the five daily ritual prayers, the monthlong fast of Ramadān, and attendance at the Friday congregational prayers); they also seek to attain deeper levels of understanding of the wisdom of the Revelation and to have "tastes" of Paradise in this lifetime.

Thus, when they speak of wine drinking, they refer not to alcohol (strictly forbidden in Islam) but to experiences of spiritual blessing, divine grace, and spiritual ecstasy, which are "tastes" of the "rivers of wine delightful to those who drink it" mentioned in the Qur'an (47:15) as a symbol of heavenly bliss. When they whirl in intensely concentrated remembrance of God, in circumambulation of the "Ka'ba of the heart," this is a mystical interpretation of the verse in the Qur'an, "Whichever way you turn, there is the Face of God" (2:115). When they quote a saying from the Prophet such as "Die before you die," they interpret it as the mystical death and transformation of egotism and an end to the obsessive preoccupation with the "idol worship" of self and worldly desires. Thus, Sufism in general, and Rumi's *Mathnawi* in particular, are inspired to a large degree by a profound and mystical understanding of the wisdom in the Qur'an and the sayings of the Prophet Muhammad.

About the Translation

I have taken a very literal approach to translating Rumi's poetry. This is in part a reaction to the proliferation of so-called translations of Rumi's poetry, which are actually interpretive poetic versions, made by authors who do not know how to read Persian (but who have used literal and accurate translations made by scholars), and which have been quite popular but are often distorted (sometimes by the addition of lines that do not appear in Rumi's original). I am not a poet, and I do not attempt to make the translations sound poetic, although I realize that this results in a pale reflection in comparison to the beauty of the meter and rhymes of the original Persian.

My aim, instead, has been to focus as best I can on the meaning of Rumi's words and teachings by studying each syllable, idiom, metaphor, and religious reference, as well as examining the explanations of commentators. And I wish to share this knowledge with lovers of Rumi's poetry who want to go beyond what the popular versions have to offer, and who are motivated to study and contemplate selections of Rumi's poetry line by line in order to gain a deeper understanding of the sublime teachings of this great mystical poet.

As a result, I have adopted the very exacting method of the British scholar R. A. Nicholson, who translated the entire *Mathnawi* more than seventy years ago by putting literal translations of Rumi's words in plain print, and then placing all additional words (needed for grammatical understanding and clarity of meaning) in parentheses. In the present book, however, the appearance of the translated texts has been made much smoother by putting all parenthetic words in italics and removing distracting parentheses.

This method preserves the integrity of Rumi's verses and allows the reader to see clearly which words are translations of Rumi's own words and which are those added by the translator. The reader may sometimes gain a richer understanding by reading the most literal words in plain print and skipping the ones in italics. I have often added such words for grammatical clarity, to smooth the flow from verse to verse, and to make the sense inherent in the Persian text (what Rumi appears to have intended or implied) more understandable in American English. Occasionally there are words in italics within brackets: these are my own added interpretations (or those of the commentators)—words that are not present in the Persian text but are supplied to make particular lines comprehensible. In such cases, further information is often added in the annotations.

To differentiate clearly between verse and prose selections from Rumi's works, the verse has been indented but the prose has not.

I am indebted to Nicholson's highly accurate translation of the *Mathnawi*, which I followed carefully for guidance as to the meaning of the verses that I have translated from Persian. Most of the cases in which my translation differs significantly from his are those that Nicholson corrected himself (in appendixes later published, as well as in his volumes of commentary).

In the case of idioms and certain other terms, translating too literally would be an error or would require excessive explanation. For example, "liver devouring" is better translated as "grievous suffering," "the two worlds" is better rendered as "this world and the next," and the common title of the Prophet, Mustafā ("the Chosen"), is translated here as Muhammad.

In regard to annotating passages from the *Mathnawi*, I have relied on the two volumes of R. A. Nicholson as well as a well-known seventeenth-century Ottoman Turkish Mevlevi commentary (translated into Persian).[23] This was the commentary that was most respected by Nicholson and was carefully followed by him when he wrote his own commentary on the *Mathnawi*. Many of Rumi's verses cannot be adequately understood and appreciated without explanations. This is also true for native Persian speakers, who may not understand Islamic references, Sufi terminology, verses in Arabic, and some classical Persian words and idioms.

When speaking about God, the Qur'an uses the Arabic pronoun "He" [*Huwa*] and describes many "Kingly" attributes of God, as well as gentle attributes such as the Beautiful, Kind, Compassionate, Forgiving, Loving, and so on. All Muslims understand that God far transcends any qualities attributed by the human mind, such as male or female. Some Muslim mystics go further by interpreting the Qur'anic term *Huwa* as the Name of the Divine Essence, which transcends all "Lordly" attributes involving the Creator's relationship to the creation. God is not referred to by the feminine pronoun in Islam, because of the absence of this usage in the Qur'an and the sayings of the Prophet, and also because of the historical conflict between the Muslims and the pagan Arabs who worshiped goddesses at Mecca. In the case of Persian, however, there is no distinction between "he," "she," and "it." This allows for an ambiguity that is common in Persian Sufi poetry: the beloved may be a beautiful woman, a handsome server of (mystical) wine, a male Sufi master with beautiful spiritual qualities, or God; the praise of the beloved's human qualities may be a symbol of praise and worship of God, or it may be praise of a human beloved and of God at the same time.

In the Qur'an, the One God speaks of Himself sometimes as "I" and sometimes as "We" or "Us." This latter is known as the plural of majesty and should not be confused with plurality of divine nature, which would be completely contrary to Islam. In Persian, the plural is similarly used in formal reverence for an individual person as well as to avoid an impolite use of the words "I" and "me" in formal situations. Thus, when Rumi uses the word "we," he often means himself; therefore, this use of the plural is usually translated here as singular.

Although most of the passages selected for this book are from Rumi's *Mathnawi*, others are taken from his other poetic works, such as his *Dīvān*, which includes his many odes and quatrains, as well as from his prose works, such as his *Discourses, Sermons,* and *Letters.*

All translations from Persian and Arabic texts of Rumi are mine. All translations of Ahādīth and verses from the Qur'an (abbreviated as Q.) are also mine, the latter having been made after consultation with several translations, chiefly those of A. Yūsuf 'Alī and Muhammad Asad.

Any readers who are interested in my other translations from Rumi's *Mathnawi* (and some of Rumi's other poetry) using the same literal approach are referred to the Dāru 'l-Masnavī website (see page 200).

Stories of the Prophet

1 This sentence was supposedly said by the Prophet whenever he returned from a battle. He also said, "Your worst enemy is your (base) self, which is between your two sides." He is said to have declared that fighting against the (base) self is the greatest warfare. This does not mean the most important warfare (after all, the small community of Muslims were in danger of being annihilated) but the most difficult. He also said, "Therefore, the strong man is the one who rules over himself during anger," and, "Truly the one who overcomes his craving is stronger than the one who conquers a city." The word *jihād* means struggle and effort, so defensive warfare against invaders and oppressors is only one aspect of "striving in God's way."

2 These verses occur in a story about a lion (which symbolizes the tyrannical ego) that is defeated by a rabbit (which symbolizes divine intelligence and guidance).

3 The craving ego is, literally, "self," but includes in Sufism the base bodily desires, vain worldly ambition, and pride—which keep the individual preoccupied with the "idol" of self and with self-will in opposition to true worship and surrender to God's Will.

4 Unbelievers are those who reject the One True God, His Prophets, righteousness and virtue, and gratitude for all the favors bestowed by the Creator. They will suffer for their denial in the Hereafter when Divine Reality is revealed to them. (See *kāfir* in the glossary.)

5 This is a reference to the Qur'anic verse regarding the Day of Judgment, "(On the) Day We will ask Hell, 'Are you filled?' And it will say, '[No], are there (any) more?'" (Q. 50:30).

1 □ Warfare

Commentary on *the saying of the Prophet*, "We have returned from the lesser warfare to the greatest warfare."[1]

O kings, we have killed the outer enemy, *but* a worse enemy than him remains in *our* interior.

Killing this *enemy* isn't the job for the rational mind and understanding, *since* the inward lion can't be compelled to work by the rabbit.[2]

This craving ego[3] is Hell, and Hell is *like* a dragon which doesn't become decreased and diminished *of its fire* by oceans.

It could drink the seven oceans, *and yet* the fiery blaze of that people-burner would still not be lessened.

Stones and stone-hearted unbelievers[4] are coming inside *of it*, groaning, crying, and ashamed.

Yet it isn't even pacified by food such as *all* this, until this call comes to it from God:

"Have you become filled, *truly* filled?"[5] *It* will say, "Still not *yet!* Look, here is fire, here is heat, here is burning [*wanting more*]!"

It ate a mouthful and consumed an *entire* world, *with* its stomach shouting, "[*No!*], are there *any* more?" (Q. 50:30).

(continued on page 5)

6 A metaphor for putting out a fire or killing a snake, which symbolizes the Omnipotence of God. According to some reported sayings of the Prophet, God will place his "Foot" on Hell, which will then cry out, "Enough, enough!" and will close its "mouth."

7 An alteration, for metrical purposes, of the verse "And when He decrees something (to be), He says to it, 'Be!' And it is" (Q. 2:117).

8 Drawing a bow is another metaphor for strength, as in an Arabic proverb according to which a champion cannot be defeated unless there is one strong enough to draw the (champion's) bowstring to match him. Here, the enemy possessing a strong bow is the base ego.

9 The greatest warfare is the struggle [*jihād*] against the base ego.

10 Qāf is the name of a mythical mountain, imagined as encircling the world and as high as the Caucasus mountains.

11 This is the prayer of the rabbit in the story (n. 2 above), who seeks to defeat the huge mountainlike lion. The image of the needle, in the context of Rumi's comments, refers to the long, difficult, and painful process of uprooting one's own selfishness and other attributes of the base ego.

From Placelessness, God will place *His* "Foot" on it[6] *and* then it will be soothed by *the words*, "'Be!' And it was."[7]

Since this craving ego of ours is part of Hell, *and since* the parts always have the nature of the whole,

Only God has the "foot" to kill it. *For no one* other than God can "draw its bow."[8]

Nothing is placed on the bow except a straight arrow, *but* this bow [*of yours only*] has arrows *that are* twisted back and crooked.

Be straight like an arrow and flee from the bow. For, undoubtedly, every *arrow which is* straight will leap *to its target.*

When I returned from the outward battle, I faced the inward battle.

"Truly, we have returned from the lesser warfare." We are together with the Prophet, *engaged* in the greatest warfare![9]

"I ask strength from God, and the favor of success and bravado, so that I may tear up this mountain of *Qāf*[10] with a needle."[11]

Consider the "lion" who breaks *through* the *battle* lines as *doing something* easy. That one is the *true* "lion" who breaks [*through the battle lines of the enemy within*] himself.

1 The captives were the prisoners of war who were captured after the first Muslim victory in battle against their polytheist enemies (who had three times the number of combatants), whose armor, weapons, and camels were then taken from them. Given hope of the Mercy of God, they later were freed, and some of them became Muslims, including the Prophet's uncle.

2 Often mistranslated by the Christian term "infidels," "rejectors" refers in the Qur'an to those who reject belief in the One God and Creator of the Universe and also reject submission to the Will of God and the authority of His Prophets and Messengers (including Abraham, Moses, Jesus, and Muhammad) who came with this message, and all that it entails.

3 "No human qualities in me": A false rumor about the Prophet, who was commanded by God, "Say, 'I am certainly a man like yourselves, (but) it has been revealed to me that your God is One God (only)'" (Q. 18:110; 41:6).

2 □ The Captives

It is coming to my mind that I should explain the *following* verse *of the* Qur'an, even though it's not connected to the *present* discussion I've spoken *about.* But since it's entered my mind *in* such a manner, I will then tell *you about it* so it may proceed.

God Most High said, "O Prophet, say to the captives[1] *who are* in your power: 'If God knows any good in your hearts, He will give you better than that which was taken from you, and He will forgive you *your sins.* And God is the Most Forgiving and Merciful'" (Q. 8:70).

The cause of the descent of this verse was *the following: Muhammad* the Chosen One—may God pour blessings upon him—*with his army* had broken *the ranks of* the rejectors *of monotheism*[2] and had killed, plundered, taken many captives, and bound *their* hands and feet. And among those prisoners, one was his uncle 'Abbās—may God be pleased with him. They were crying and wailing the entire night in *their* fetters, helplessness, and wretched humiliation. They were severed of *all* hope for themselves and were expecting the sword and execution. Muhammad—may the blessings *of God* be upon him—gazed at them and laughed.

They thought he was laughing because of conquering them, and they said to one another, "Did you see that there are human qualities in him *after all?* So that which he was claiming—'There are no human qualities in me'[3]—isn't *true,* and was the opposite of the truth. Look! He gazes at us and sees us, *who are* in fetters and neck chains, as his captives. *And* he becomes happy—just like those *who are* driven by egotism and *worldly* cravings: when they have obtained victory over their enemies, they become happy looking at those who are their captives. And they are thrilled with joy."

(continued on page 9)

7

4 According to a saying of the Prophet, "Our Lord was amazed concerning a people (who are) dragged toward Paradise in chains."

Muhammad—may God pour blessings upon him—understood their thoughts *and* said, "No! *God* forbid that I should laugh because I see enemies as conquered by me and become happy because of that! Rather, my laughter is involved with this: that I'm seeing, with the eye *which views what is* secret, that I'm dragging and pulling a people by force from the *blazing* furnace and chimney *filled* with the black smoke of Hell—toward Paradise, the Angel who guards the Heavenly Gates, and the everlasting Garden. And they are in *a state of* groaning and clamoring, saying, 'Why are you taking us from this dangerous place into that garden and place of safety?'[4] *So* laughter takes hold of me.

"But all this *aside*, since you still lack the vision to see clearly and to understand what I am talking about, God Most High says, 'Tell these captives: "First you joined armies together with a great multitude and magnificence, and you displayed complete trust in your manly courage and heroism. You told yourselves, 'We will do it like this. We will defeat the Muslims and we will conquer *them.*' *But* you did not see anyone more powerful than you, and you did not understand *that there is* an All-Subduing One above your *own power to* force. Therefore, everything that you planned to do—saying, 'It will happen like this,' became entirely the opposite. Again, even now that you are left in *a state of* fear, you have not repented of that ailment and have become hopeless, since you do not see an All-Powerful One above you. Therefore, it is necessary that you see My Strength and Majesty immediately, and to know that you are conquered by Me, so that all matters may become easy *for you.* And also, do not sever hope of [*help from*] Me in *your* state of fear. For I am able to free you from this fear and make you safe. The One who brought forth a black bull from a white cow is also able to bring forth a white bull from a black cow, *just as in the verses,* 'He turns the night into day, and He turns the day into night' (Q. 35:13), and 'He brings forth the living from what is dead, and He brings forth the dead from

(continued on page 11)

5 True faith is remembering God in all situations, such as when fearing temptation to sin, facing danger and loss, or hoping for right guidance, safety, and gain (thereby seeking protection or benefit from God alone).

6 In another discourse, Rumi relates that the Prophet's heart was afflicted with compassion for the captives when the Revelation to the captives came, which he interprets: "In this condition of fetters and chains that you are in, if you make the intention to do good and righteous actions, God Most High will free you from these bonds. And He will give back that which has gone (from you)—and many times that. And (He will grant you) forgiveness, and Paradise in the Afterlife— and (He will give you) two treasures: one which has (now) gone from you and one treasure of the Hereafter."

7 'Abbās had been a polytheist but went on to become an important Muslim, whose descendants ruled the 'Abbāsid dynasty, from the year 749 c.e. until the Mongol army destroyed Baghdad in 1258.

8 In the continuation of this story, when the Prophet's uncle was asked to give all his wealth and possessions to the Muslim cause, he claimed he had nothing left, and the Prophet clairvoyantly told him where he had hidden his wealth. Finally his uncle became truthful and his acceptance of the Faith sincere. Elsewhere, Rumi relates that one night the Prophet felt pain in his hands and he received a revelation that this was the effect of the pain in his uncle's hands from being bound (too tightly).

9 Rumi comments here with a poetic verse.

what is living' (Q. 30:19). Now, in this situation *in* which you are captive, do not sever hope of My Presence, so that I may take your hands.
Since, 'truly, no one despairs of the Comforting Mercy of God except
the rejectors' (Q. 12:87)."

"Now, God Most High is telling *you*, 'O captives! If you turn back
from your original creed and look toward Me in *states of* fear and hope,[5]
and view yourselves in every condition as conquered by My Might, I
will free you from this fear. And every possession which has gone from
you and become lost by *being seized as* plunder, I will give all *back* to you.
Rather, I will double it *manifold*, I will forgive you, and I will join the good
fortune of the next world to that of the *present* world *for you*.'"[6]

The Prophet's Uncle 'Abbās[7] said, "I've repented and I've turned back
from that which I was. Muhammad—may God's blessings be upon
him said, 'God Most High seeks a sign *of proof* from you regarding
this claim *of yours*.'"[8]

Making the claim of love is easy,
but there must be proof of it.[9]

1 Another story tells of Bilāl, the freed black slave who was chosen by the Prophet to be the first announcer of the call to prayer for each of the five daily ritual prayers. See chapter 5.

2 Hilāl literally means "New Moon." He was a devoted Muslim of exceptional spiritual understanding and chose to remain as the slave and groom of a wealthy commander who was also a Muslim convert, but spiritually blind.

3 This relates to the saying of the Prophet "Die before you die," interpreted by the Sufis as the death of ego and its dominance.

4 "Pious" refers to someone of exceptional religious faith, as defined by the Prophet: "Piety is worshiping God as if you have seen Him; for truly, if you don't see Him, He certainly sees you."

3 □ Hilāl

Since you have listened to a few of the *good* qualities of Bilāl,[1] now listen to the story of the weakened *state* of Hilāl.[2]

He was greater *in spiritual rank* on the *spiritual* Way than Bilāl, *since* he had done more to kill *his* bad nature.[3]

How this Hilāl became sick and the lack of awareness of his master regarding his illness, because of contempt and lack of recognition *of his value.* And *how* the heart of Muhammad—upon him be peace—became aware of his illness and *his* condition. And *how* the Prophet—upon him be peace—investigated and visited this Hilāl.

By *divine* decree, Hilāl became sick and unwell. Inspiration *from God* became, for Muhammad, the tale bearer of *his* condition.

His [*prominent and wealthy*] master lacked awareness of his illness, since, for him, *Hilāl* was uninteresting and not in danger.

A pious man[4] *was* sick in the stable for nine days, and no person was ever aware of his condition.

Yet, the one who was a person and *also* the Emperor of *all* persons, whose mind reached everywhere like a hundred Red Seas—

Inspiration came to him: the Mercy of God was sympathetic, saying, "Such-and-such a yearning one of yours has become sick."

Muhammad went *in* that direction for the sake of visiting the sick, for the sake of the honorable Hilāl.

(continued on page 15)

5   The Prophet said, "My Companions are like the stars; whichever of them you follow, you will be (rightly) guided."

6   Meteors are depicted in the Qur'an (67:5) as driving away devils who sneak too close to the borders of Heaven.

7   "Scattering his own soul" is an idiom of self-sacrificing generosity, in a similar manner of scattering coins.

8   The greeting of peace is in Arabic: "May the peace (of God) be upon you" [*as-salāmu 'alaykum*]. The reply is "And may the peace (of God) be upon you (also)" [*wa 'alaykuma 's-salām*]. It remains the customary greeting of Muslims all over the world.

9   This holy phrase [bi'smi 'llāh] is used by Muslims when beginning any activity, practice, or journey.

10   "The spiritual Axis" is a Sufi term, meaning the spiritual master who is the "spiritual pole" of the age, around which all other spiritual masters revolve. Here, the Prophet is viewed in even loftier terms.

11   He revealed his self-centered (and blind) arrogance.

12   "New Moon" is the meaning of the slave's Arabic name.

13   That is, secretly perceiving what is in people's hearts.

That "Moon" was running behind the Sun of inspiration, and the Companions *came* after him, like stars.

The "Moon" says, "My Companions are *like* stars:[5] an example for night travelers *to follow*, and meteors[6] for *driving away* insolent oppressors."

The master was told, "That *spiritual* king has arrived." He leaped up, faint of heart and soul because of joy.

Based on *his* presumption about that *arrival*, he clapped both hands in happiness, *believing* that the *spiritual* Emperor had come for the sake of *visiting* the master.

When that master came down from *his* upper room, he was scattering *his own* soul[7] as a reward to a messenger of good news.

Then he kissed the ground *in front of the Prophet* and presented the *greeting of* peace.[8] He made his *own* face *as cheerful* as a rose, out of joy.

He said, "In the name of God,[9] give honor *to this* home so that this place of gathering may become a paradise,

"*And* so that my great house may extend above the heavens *in grandeur*, saying *to itself*, 'I saw the *spiritual* Axis[10] *around which* Time rotates.'"

That revered *Prophet* told him, for the sake of reprimand, "I haven't come for the sake of meeting you."

The master said, "My spirit *is* yours! What is the *value of my* spirit *in your presence?* Oh, *please* tell *me* for whose sake *you have undertaken* this burden,

"So that I may be the dust *under* the feet of *such* a person who is planted in the ground of the orchard of your grace."

When he said this and drove *his* pride *into the open*,[11] Muhammad *by way of* discontinuing his rebuke, spoke.

And then told him, "Where is that New Moon[12] of the most lofty heaven? Where *the one who is* spread out like moonbeams *on the ground* out of humility?

"*Where is* that king *who has* been hidden in *a state of* slavery *and who has* come *down* to this world for the sake of spying?[13]

"Don't say, 'He is my slave and stable worker.' Know this: he is a treasure *buried* in ruins.

(continued on page 17)

14 According to the Qur'anic account, before the Prophet Joseph's shirt was brought by his brothers from Egypt to his father, the Prophet Jacob, the latter said, "Truly I smell the presence of Joseph" (12:94).

15 One of Rumi's main teachings is that beings who have similar qualities have attraction to each other. He says elsewhere, "Because commonality is a wonderful attractor; wherever there is a seeker, a kindred spirit is his attractor. Jesus and Enoch [*Idrīs*] went up to the Heavens because they were kindred spirits with the angels."

16 This refers especially to miracles done to punish the deniers of the One True God, such as the plagues sent to Egypt (Q. 7:133) and the drowning of Pharaoh and his followers (Q. 2:50) so that the Children of Israel could escape bondage.

"Oh dread! How is that New Moon Hilāl *affected* by illness, *the one by* whom thousands of full moons are crushed *under his* feet?"

The master replied, "I don't have news of his illness, but he isn't at the *front* gate—for several days *now.*

"His company is with the horses and mules. He's a groom, and his dwelling place is the stable."

About the coming of Muhammad—upon him be peace—to the stable of that master for the sake of visiting Hilāl, and about Muhammad's soothing of Hilāl—may God be pleased with him.

The Prophet went into the stable for his sake with *a feeling* of affection and began looking and searching *for him.*

The stable was dark, hideous, and dirty. *However,* all this disappeared when friendship arrived.

That *spiritual* lion smelled the Prophet's scent, just as the scent of Joseph *was smelled* by his father.[14]

Miracles are not the cause of faith *in God, but it is* the scent of commonality[15] *that* causes the *attraction* of *similar* qualities.

The miracles *of the* Prophets are for the sake of overcoming the enemy,[16] *whereas* the scent of commonality is for winning the heart.

The enemy is conquered, but not a friend. A friend is never made by being bound by the neck.

Hilāl came into *consciousness* from sleep because of *the Prophet's* scent *and* said *to himself,* "A place full of dung *and* a scent of this kind within it!"

From between the legs of the riding animals, he saw the holy robe of the Prophet without equal.

Then he came crawling from the corner of the stable, *and* that *spiritual* knight placed *his* face upon *the Prophet's* feet.

Then the Prophet placed *his* face upon *Hilāl's* face and gave him kisses upon his head, eyes, and cheeks.

(continued on page 19)

17 Here, the Prophet acknowledges that Hilāl is a hidden saint, unrecognized by most. The words "hidden pearl" is a Persian translation of the Qur'anic image of handsome male servants in Paradise (one of many symbols of heavenly bliss) who are "like hidden pearls" (52:24, 56:23). Elsewhere, Rumi uses the term "hidden pearl" to symbolize hidden spiritual knowledge of great value (see *Math.*, I:2390; V:2794).

And he said, "O Lord! What a hidden pearl[17] you are! How are you, O stranger from the highest heaven? Are you better?

Hilāl replied, "How is the one with disturbed sleep, when *the light* of the sun arrives to his mouth?

"How is the thirsty person who chews *moist* clay *in order to survive,* when *flood* water places him on top *of itself* and carries *him* away happily?

"*And how is* the blind man *who has been* going on *his* stomach like a snake, *when his* eyes opened to *the sight of* the garden and *the beauty of* the Spring?"

1 This Arabic phrase is used when one mentions the names of any of the Prophets, from Adam, Seth, and Noah to Moses, Jesus, and Abraham.

2 The gentle and compassionate character of Muhammad is famous among Muslims but little known to most Westerners.

3 Visiting the sick is considered a duty and a virtue rewarded by God. There are many sayings of the Prophet related to the duty and blessing of visiting the sick.

4 A pole of the saints is the chief in the Sufi hierarchy of saints.

5 A great spiritual king means a hidden Sufi saint who has God-given powers, and thus compared to a king [shāh].

6 "Eyes of the heart": Here, discrimination between good and evil.

7 A traditional saying is that treasures are buried underneath ruined buildings and sites.

8 A dervish is someone who is humble before God, usually used for a Sufi, or practitioner of Islamic mysticism.

9 A friend of the mystical path is a Sufi whose contact may be beneficial.

4 □ The Sick One

About the going of Muhammad—may peace of God be upon him[1]—to visit a sick companion. And an explanation of the *spiritual* benefit of visiting the sick.

A prominent man among the companions *of Muhammad* became sick. And in that sickness of his, he became like a thread *in thinness.*

Muhammad came to him *for the benefit of* visiting the sick, since his character was entirely kindness and generosity.[2]

There is benefit in your going to visit the sick,[3] *and the benefit of* that is returning back to you.

The first and foremost benefit *is* that the ill person may perhaps be a pole *of the saints*[4] and a great *spiritual* king.[5]

But since you don't have the two eyes of the heart,[6] O stubborn one—because you don't know *how* "firewood" *is different* from *fragrant* "aloes" *wood*—

Don't be distressed, since a "treasure" exists in the world. So don't consider any ruined place empty of treasure.[7]

Make *it your* intention *to visit* any dervish[8] randomly. If you find the sign [*of saintliness*], make an effort to circle round *that one.*

Since eyes *capable* of seeing inwardly weren't *given* to you, keep imagining that the "treasure" *may be* in every person.

And if he isn't a pole *of the saints,* he may be a friend of the *mystical* path.[9] *And* if he isn't a "king," he may be a "knight" *in charge* of mounted troops.

So consider relationship with the friends of the Way as indispensable—whoever it is, whether a "foot soldier" or a "mounted knight."

(continued on page 23)

10 Rumi advises us to strive with devotion to make friends with all Sufis and to see their inner spiritual qualities.

11 This may refer to sayings of the Prophet Muhammad, such as "The (helping) Hand of God is with the gathering (of believers)."

12 Rumi means the possible beneficial relationship with someone who may be a hidden (spiritual) "king," perhaps in the guise of a poor beggar.

13 This refers to a saying (piously but incorrectly) attributed by the Sufis to the Prophet: "The one who wants to sit together with God should sit together with the people of Sufism."

14 A protective shadow (like that attributed to a king, as the "Shadow of God on earth") that strengthens spiritual determination and discipline and may give the disciple more and more spiritual blessings.

15 Travel with dervishes and supporters of the Islamic Sufi path.

And if he is an enemy, this kindness is equally good, since many enemies have become friends by *being treated with* kindness.

And if he doesn't become a friend, his hatred will become less, because kind and generous treatment is the healing ointment for hatred and ill will.

There are many benefits other than these, but I'm fearful of being *too* lengthy, O good friend.

The summary has been this: be the friend of the congregation [*of those who seek God*]. Chisel a friend out of stone,[10] like an idol maker.

Since a crowd and congregation[11] of *those belonging to* a caravan will break the backs and spears of highway robbers.

⌘

The return to the story of the sick man and the visiting of the Prophet—may the peace *of God* be upon him.

This visiting of the sick is for this *spiritual* connection,[12] and this relationship is pregnant with a hundred loving friendships.

The Prophet, *who had* no equal, went to visit the sick *man, and* he saw a companion in the state of *undergoing* death's agonies.

If you become distant from the presence of the saints,[13] you've been distant from God, in reality.

Since the consequence of separation from traveling companions is sadness and anguish, separation from the faces *of spiritual* kings is never less than that.

So hurry every moment in search of the *protecting* shadow of *spiritual* kings, so that you may become more excellent than the sun by means of that shadow.[14]

If you have a journey *ahead of you,* go with this intention;[15] and if *your* staying present *at home* is *to continue,* don't be neglectful of this *intention.*

∞

(*continued on page 25*)

16 Close companion means, literally, "Friend of the Cave," which is a title of honor given to the closest companion, disciple, and first successor of the Prophet, Abu Bakr, who hid with him in a cave when pagan enemies were searching for the Prophet during his famous escape from Mecca to Medina, intending to kill him.

17 The sick man refers to the Islamic practice of rising in the middle of the night and doing extra ritual prayers. This was practiced by the Prophet and advocated in the Qur'an: "And strive to keep vigil for part of the night an additional prayer for you" (Q. 17:79; see also 25:64, 51:15–18). Muslim mystics, or Sufis, also do additional litanies and chanting of the praises of God at this time, or preceding the predawn ritual prayer.

18 A basic teaching of Rumi is that Divine Mercy is hidden beneath the trials, misfortunes, and suffering that result from the divine attribute of Severity.

19 The fountain of eternal youth, a fabled spring of water said to confer immortality to the one who drinks from it, is a frequent metaphor in Rumi's poetry.

20 Rumi refers to a type of "death" in this lifetime, in which the mystic escapes the obsessive preoccupations with ego and ego-based desires.

About the knowing of the Prophet—may the peace *of God* be upon him—that the cause of the illness of that person was insolent boldness in prayer.

When the Prophet saw the sick man, he acted soothingly and kindly toward that close companion.[16]

And when he saw the Prophet, he became enlivened; you could say that *the Prophet's holy* breath created him *anew.*

He said, "Sickness gave me this good fortune—that this king came to *visit* me at dawn,

"*And* so that health and recovery have reached me by the arrival of this king, *who came* without attendants.

"O fortunate agony, sickness, and fever! O blessed pain and sleeplessness at night!

"Now God has given me an illness and ailment in my old age out of *His* kindness and generosity.

"He has also given backaches, so that, inevitably, I leap up quickly every *time in the* middle of the night—

"God has given me pain, out of His kindness and grace, so that I won't sleep *through* the entire night[17] like a buffalo.

"By account of this being broken *down,* the mercy of *spiritual* kings has surged *up, and* Hell has been made silent from *making* threats to me."

Pain became a treasure [*for that sick man*], because there are mercies within it.[18] The *fruity* pulp became fresh *only* when you scraped *off* the rind.

O brother, [*suffering*] a dark and cold place *and* practicing enduring patience with grief, weakness, and suffering—

That is the Fountain of *Everlasting* Life[19] and the cup of *spiritual* drunkenness, for those *spiritual* heights are entirely *derived* from *humble* lowliness.

Those Spring-seasons are hidden in the Fall, *and* that Fall-season is *latent* in the Spring—don't run from it.

Be a traveling companion with sorrow and adjust to dread; seek long life [*in Paradise*] through your own [*ego*] death.[20]

(*continued on page 27*)

21 The word *nafs* (ego) includes the bodily or "animal" self with its cravings, negative emotions, the opinionated and prideful intellect, as well as the illusion of separate selfhood that leads to "worshiping self" instead of God and obeying self-will instead of God's Will.

22 Rumi refers to an incident in the life of the Prophet: "When God showed them [the pagan enemies] in your dream as small (in number); for if He had shown them as many, you would have become faint-hearted" (Q. 8:43).

23 "The outward and inner struggle and battle" can mean defensive warfare against oppressors and invaders (see Q. 22:39–40; 2:190; 4:74–75) as well as struggle against the selfish desires of the base ego (see *jihād* in the glossary).

24 This line includes terms from the Qur'an having to do with hardship and ease sent by God. (See, for "ease," Q. 18:88, 65:4, 7; 94:5–6; for "hardship," Q. 92:10, 65:7, 94:5, 6.)

25 God made the Muslims to appear as few in number to the invading pagan army, which was vastly greater but was defeated at the Battle of Badr near Medina (see Q. 8:44).

26 This refers to a sword used by the Prophet, who gave it to his cousin and son-in-law, 'Ali.

As for that which your ego[21] is telling *you*: "This place *of suffering* is bad"—don't listen to it, since its actions have been opposed [*to your spiritual freedom*].

You should oppose it, for this same advice has come from *all* the Prophets in the world.

Your ego is the deceptive ocean *which has* revealed *only* some foam; it is the Hell *which,* from deceit, *has* shown *only* a *bit of* flame.

In your eyes, it appears *to be* small so that you may see it as lowly and weak *and so that* your anger may be roused *against it.*

Just as *when* there was a large army *of pagan enemies,* to the Prophet, it appeared in *his* eyes as small,[22]

So that the Prophet rushed at them without *concern for* danger. For if he had seen them as exceeding *the number of his fighters,* he would have acted with caution and avoidance.

That was the favor and grace *of God.* And you were worthy of it, O Muhammad, for otherwise you would have become weak-hearted and timid.

For him and his companions, God made the outward and inner struggle and battle[23] to appear *as something* small and minor,

So that He made attainment and success easy for him, and *so that* He made him turn *his* face away from difficulty[24] *best avoided.*

Victory was *the result of* the *danger* appearing small to him, since God was his friend and teacher of the way *to success.*

But regarding the one for whom God is not his support in victory, sorrow *for him* if the virile lion appears *like* a cat to him!

Misery *for him,* if he sees a hundred *enemies* from afar as a single one,[25] so that he enters the battle out of vain conceit and false hope!

By means of that *One,* a blessed sword[26] appears as a *mere* dagger; because of that *One,* a virile lion appears as a *mere* cat—

(continued on page 29)

27 Zoroastrian fire-worship is used as an example of false worship of other than the One True God. Here, "fire temple" is a symbol of Hell-fire.

28 That is, they went astray by their own choice.

29 "Stem" refers to the Prophets and saints, who may appear weak and rejected but who are actually "spiritual kings."

30 'Āj, the son of 'Unuq, refers to a legend about a giant, who was killed by Moses.

31 This is the story told in the Book of Exodus and mentioned in the Qur'an (2:50).

32 An ancient belief that an evil supernatural being (called *ghūl* in Arabic) may lurk on the side of a road and attempt to lure travelers to their doom is used here as a metaphor for the voice of Satan.

33 The Prophet asks whether the sick man may have spoken out of foolishness and lack of proper reverence toward God.

So that fools may plunge bravely into combat, and He may deliver them to the *seizing* grasp *of the victors;*

And so that those foolish ones will have come to the fire-temple[27] by *means of* their own *two* feet.[28]

He brings the stem of a leaf into view, so that you may *try to* blow it out of existence *with your breath.*

But take care! Since that "stem"[29] has torn away mountains *and* the world *has been* weeping because of it, while *the stem* is in *a state of* laughter.

He makes the river water appear *as if it were only* up to the ankles, *but* a hundred like *the giant named* 'Āj the son of 'Unuq[30] have been drowned by it.

He makes a wave of blood appear to him *like* a pile of musk, *and* He makes the bottom of the sea appear *like* dry land.

Blind Pharaoh viewed that sea *as* dry *land*,[31] so that he drove *his army into it with all his* manliness and strength.

So when he comes in, he's at the bottom of the sea. How can the eyes of Pharaoh *be expected to* be *clear* seeing?

The eyes become *truly* seeing by means of meeting with God, *for* God never becomes a secret-sharing friend with any foolish person.

The fool sees what is actually deadly poison *as if it is* candy, *and* he sees what is actually the call of the ghoul[32] *as if it is* the *true* road.

The remainder of the advice given to the sick man by the Prophet—may the peace of God *be* upon him.

While he had visited his miserable friend *further,* the Prophet said to the sick man,

"Perhaps you have made some kind of prayer *and* 'eaten' something poisonous out of ignorance?[33]

"Bring to memory what prayer you may have said when you were *feeling* disturbed by the deception of *your* ego."

(continued on page 31)

34 The man asks Muhammad to direct a strong beneficial spiritual influence toward him by means of prayerful concentration.

35 This is an Arabic idiom used for someone who interferes in what is
not his business.

36 He refers to sermons by the Prophet, warning his followers against
indulging in sins.

37 Rumi comments on a story (not in the Qur'an) of how the angels of
Heaven bragged that they were superior to Adam, and God led two
of them into temptation on earth. After seducing a beautiful woman
in exchange for words of power, the two angels requested to be punished on earth by being hung by their legs in a pit in Babylon, to avoid
facing punishment for their actions on the Day of Judgment.

38 This is another use of the word *jihād* in the sense of striving against
the self-centered desires of ego.

The sick man replied, "I have no memory *of it,* but keep a favorable will toward me,[34] *so that* the memory may reach me in a while."

Because of the light-bestowing presence of Muhammad, that prayer of his came before his mind.

The light which is the discrimination between truth and falsehood shone through the window which is between heart and heart.

He said, "Now the memory has come *back,* O Prophet—the prayer which I, the father of foolish meddling,[35] *had* spoken.

"*Once* when I was the captive of sin, *and* drowning *with my* hands lunging at straws,

"*When* some warnings and threats about very severe punishments for sinners was coming from you,[36]

"*And* I was becoming disturbed and upset, there was no remedy *in sight,* the shackles were *fastened* tightly, and the lock wasn't *able to be* opened

"*There was* no place for patience, no way of escape, no hope of repentance, *and* nowhere to fight.

"Because of *such* sorrow and sadness, I was like *the fallen angels* Hārūt and Mārūt: I kept sighing, 'O my Creator!'"

Hārūt and Mārūt[37] openly chose *to be imprisoned in* the pit of Babylon, because of the danger *of facing the Day of Judgment,*

So that they might suffer here the punishment of the Afterlife; and they are shrewd and intelligent, and resemble magicians.

They behaved well and were *adjusted* to their place *of confinement, for* the misery of smoke is easier *to bear* than *that of* fire.

"There is no limit or description of the suffering of that *future* world; the suffering of *this* world is easy *when placed* before it.

"O blessed is the one who keeps making effort and struggle[38] *by* applying prohibitions and justice toward *the desires of* the body,

"*And who* places upon himself the pains of worshiping and serving God so that he may escape from the pain of that *future* world!

(continued on page 33)

39 The word for remembrance, recollection, and mentioning the praises of God is used [*zikr,* also spelled *dhikr*], a word and practice mentioned numerous times in the Qur'an (such as 33:41, 3:41, 7:205, 4:103, 13:28, 24:37, 59:19, 9:67, 29:45). Muslim mystics, or Sufis, have specialized in practicing the remembrance, praise, and glorification of God as much as possible.

40 "Assigned litanies" refers to selections from the Qur'an assigned by a Sufi master to disciples, together with chanting names of God (in Arabic), usually every morning.

41 The followers of Muhammad are compared to the Children of Israel, who wandered for years in circles in the desert.

42 He refers to the miracle of how God provided manna from the Heavens to the Children of Israel (Q. 2:57, 7:160).

"I kept saying, 'O Lord, send forth quickly that *future* punishment upon me in this world also,

"'So that there may be rest and ease for me in that *next* world.' I was knocking the door ring *of Heaven while* supplicating in such a manner.

"*Then* a *terrible* sickness such as this manifested to me, *and* my soul has been without rest because of the pain *ever since.*

"I've been kept from *being able to practice* remembrance *of God*[39] and my assigned litanies;[40] I've *also* been unaware of myself *and of* good and bad.

"If I hadn't seen your face now—Oh *how* fortunate and oh *how* blessed is your scent!—

"I would have gone completely from the bonds [*of my body*]. But you have given me this sympathetic care in a royal manner."

The Prophet said, "Take care! Don't make this prayer again! Don't tear out yourself from root and stem.

"O weak ant, what strength do you have for enduring such a tall mountain which He might place upon you?"

The sick man replied, "I have repented, O king: I won't talk nonsense in any *such* manner from extreme rashness *again!*

"This world is *like* the wilderness *of the Children of Israel,* you are *like* Moses *to us,* and we *have* been left in the desert *in a state of* trial and affliction because of *our* sins.

"We are traveling the way for years, and finally *we continue to remain* captive in the first halting place *of the journey;*

"The people of Moses[41] have been traversing the way, and in the end have been at the first step.

"If the heart of Moses were satisfied and pleased with us, the way *through* the desert and *to its* border would have been revealed.

"But if he were completely fed up with us, trays of food would never have reached us from heaven;[42]

(continued on page 35)

43 This is another famous miracle worked by God through the Prophet Moses, mentioned in the Qur'an (2:60, 7:160).

44 "Give good to us": This is in Arabic and a metrical adaptation of a famous Qur'anic prayer, "Give good to us, (O) our Lord, in this world and (also) good in the Hereafter, and protect us from the punishment of the Fire (of Hell)!" (2:201). Here, it means health and well-being in this world and forgiveness and Paradise in the next.

45 Being with God (in Paradise) is the only true goal.

46 Muslims are the (true) believers. This term, broadly understood, can include monotheists who follow previous scriptures (see Q. 5:72).

47 The Qur'anic word is used, which means rejectors of the One God, deniers of the revelations brought by the Prophets, and those who are ungrateful for all the blessings of their Creator. (See *kāfir* in the glossary.)

48 This refers to a Qur'anic verse referring to Hell-fire, "And truly (there are none) of you but will pass by it" (Q. 19:71).

49 God will speak to the believers through the angels.

50 Here is another instance of the word *jihād* used to mean "striving against selfishness and egotism."

51 "Piety" is a Qur'anic term important in Islam and Islamic mysticism (Sufism), which means reverential awe toward God, a type of fear related to love, and an aversion to risk displeasing God. It is a consciousness of the Presence of God that inspires the believer to cultivate virtues such as righteousness, compassion, forgiveness, patient endurance, kindness, and generosity.

"Fountains of water would never have surged from any rocks;[43] there would never have been any safety and security for our lives in the desert."

About the giving of advice by the Prophet—may the peace of God *be* upon him—to that sick man and teaching him to pray.

The Prophet told the sick man, "Say this: 'O You *who* make difficulties easy,

"'Give good to us[44] in our abode in *this* world and give good to us in our abode in the following *world*.

"'Make the way like a garden, fair and exquisite to us! *For* You Yourself are our *final* halting place,[45] O Holy and Glorious One!'"

At the Gathering *on the Day of Judgment*, the *true* believers[46] will say, "O angel, isn't it *true* that Hell is *to be* a shared road,

"*And that both true* believers and unbelievers[47] will find *their* passageway *to be* next to it?[48] *But* we didn't see *any* smoke or fire on this road.

"Look! *This is* Paradise and the *Divine* Court of safety and protection, *so* where was that base and contemptible passageway?"

Then the angel will say,[49] "That 'meadow of green herbs' which you have seen in such-and-such a place while passing—

"That was Hell and the place of severe punishment, *but* to you it was *in the appearance* of orchards, gardens, and trees.

"Since *in regard to* this Hell-natured ego—*this* fiery fire-worshiper *and* seeker of temptation, rebellion, and calamity—

"You have made struggles and combats[50] *against it*, you have extinguished *its* fire for the sake of God, *and* it has become full of purity and serenity;

"*Since* the fire of excessive desire and lust, which you were *formerly* setting ablaze, has become the garden of piety[51] and the light of *divine* guidance;

(continued on page 37)

52   That is, he has followed the guidance of the Prophet through his sayings and deeds.

53   Here, Rumi inserts a comment in his own voice.

54   "Is there a reward for doing good, besides (receiving) good?" (Q. 55:60).

55   "Annihilated...everlasting" refers to two Sufi terms that are based on the Qur'anic verse "All that is upon (the earth) will pass away, but the Face of your Lord will abide, full of majesty and Glory" (Q. 55:26–27).

56   The goblet is filled with spiritual bliss, not alcohol, which is forbidden in Islam.

57   "His Word and Command" means the Holy Qur'an.

58   That is, waging and gambling away one's life for the sake of God.

59   "The Friend" is a Persian term, which may also be translated as "the Beloved"—the loving, caring, guiding qualities of God.

"*Since* the fire of anger from *within* you has also become patient restraint *and* the darkness of ignorance from *within* you has become *spiritual* knowledge;

"*Since* the fire of greed from *within* you has become abundant generosity *and* that envy *which* was like thorns has become a rose garden;

"*Since* you have previously extinguished all of these *inner* fires of yours for the sake of God,

"*And* made *your* fiery ego like an orchard, and tossed the seeds of faithfulness *to* God into it,

"*So that* nightingales of remembrance *of God* and glorification *of Him* have been singing sweetly within it, in the meadow beside the river;

"*Since* you have answered the caller to God[52] you have brought water into the *burning* Hell of *your* ego—

"In regard to you, Our Hell has also become a green meadow, rose gardens, provision, and plenty."

O son,[53] what is the reward for doing good?[54] Kindness, benevolence, and honored *spiritual* reward.

[*The angel said*], "Didn't you say, 'We are a sacrifice to God *and* we are annihilated in the presence of His everlasting Attributes'?[55]

[*"And you also said"*], 'Whether we are sly and crafty or crazy, we are drunk with that cupbearer and that goblet *of wine*.[56]

"'We are *reverently* placing our heads upon His Word and Command,[57] *and* we are offering our sweet lives in pledge *to Him*.[58]

"'Since the thought of the Friend[59] is in our innermost consciousness, our duty is service *to Him* and offering up our lives.'"

(*continued on page 39*)

60 Rumi comments in his own voice.

61 "The face of the friend" is a metaphor for the light-giving spiritual master, who in turn is a symbol for God.

62 This refers to "the friends of God," a Qur'anic term used by the Sufis to refer to the holy saints.

63 That is, full of spiritual blessings, serenity, and bliss.

64 "Make your dwelling in the Heavens": Beyond the dimensions of the physical world, as well as within the "heavenly abode" of the souls and hearts of the saints.

Wherever the candle of trial and affliction has been lit, hundreds of thousands of loving souls have been burnt.[60]

For any lovers *of God* who are intimate companions are *like* moths at the candle of the face of the friend.[61]

O heart, go where they are shining toward you[62] and are an armored coat *of protection* for you from trial and affliction;

Where they may console *you* for your sins and offenses, *and where* they may make a place for you in the midst of *their* souls;

And where they may make a place for your soul within that midst, so that they may make you full of wine like a goblet.[63]

Take *your* home in the midst of their souls! O shining full moon, make your dwelling in the Heavens![64]

1 God looks at what is inward, not what is outward.

2 Many Muslim mystics, or Sufis, emphasize God as the Beloved and Source of Love.

3 Strangers are those who are more distant from God and whose hearts are distant from true lovers of God.

4 Bilāl was an African Muslim from Ethiopia, a slave who was freed after converting to Islam. He was chosen by the Prophet to be the first to recite the famous Islamic call to prayer. The Prophet used to say, "O Bilāl, revive us (with the call to) prayer."

5 As an Ethiopian, Bilāl was unable to recite the more guttural "H" in Arabic; he could say it only by using the other "H," easily pronounced but resulting in an unintelligible word.

6 The mu'azzin recites the "call to prayer" [azān] in a loud voice five times a day, usually from the minaret of a mosque.

7 That is, the beginning of the era of the religion of Islam.

8 The complete call to prayer is a set of phrases repeated twice (except for the last one): "God is Most Great," "There is no divinity but (the One) God," "Muhammad is the Messenger of God," "Come to the prayer," "Come to prosperity and salvation," "God is Most Great," "There is no divinity but (the One) God."

5 □ Bilāl

If your speech is distorted *but* your meaning is right *in prayer,*[1] that distorted expression is acceptable and pleasing to God.

In **explanation that, for** *God* **the Beloved,**[2] **a mistake** *done* **by the lovers** *of God* **is better than the correct action of strangers.**[3]

While *making* the call to ritual prayer in *a state of* humble supplication, that truthful Bilāl[4] kept reciting the word "Come [*Hayya*] to prayer!" incorrectly as "hayya,"[5]

Until *some* said, "O Messenger *of God,* a mistake *such as* this isn't right now—*especially* when it is the beginning of the foundation *of Islam.*

"O Prophet! And O Messenger of the Creator! Bring *forth for us* a prayer-caller[6] who is more fluent and correct.

"*During* the beginning of *true* religion and virtue,[7] reciting wrongly the expression 'Come to prosperity and salvation!'[8] is a shame."

(continued on page 13)

9 The Prophet intuitively understood the special blessings that Bilāl had received from God.

10 The Prophet had intuitive knowledge of the hidden sins and fault of these objectors and of the future consequences to their souls.

11 Rumi gives his interpretation of the essential meaning of the story for his listeners: Don't criticize those who are saintly and holy, but ask them to pray to God for your sake instead. This also refers to a saying of the Prophet: "The prayer of someone (who is) absent for someone (who is also) not present (with him) is more quickly answered."

The Prophet's anger surged up, and he uttered one or two hints about the hidden favors *received by Bilāl,*[9]

Saying, "O low-minded ones, in regard to God, Bilāl's *badly pronounced* 'hayy' is superior to hundreds of *correctly uttered words such as* 'Hayy' and 'khayy' or *any other* word or expression.

"Don't make me upset, so that I won't speak openly *about* your secrets—your end and beginning."[10]

If you lack a sweet breath in *saying* prayers, go and ask for a prayer from the pure brothers *of the heart.*[11.]

A large group of Arabs (including some Kurds, as the story later reveals) were transporting merchandise on camels along a trade route.

Literally, "the Chosen" [*Mustafā*] Prophet of God.

6 □ The Water Carrier

The story of *how* the Prophet—may the peace *of God* be upon him—responded to the call for help *made by* a caravan of Arabs[1] who were in despair from thirst and lack of water, and *who* had settled *their* hearts upon *the expectation of* death. *And how both the camels and people had cast their tongues from their mouths because of thirst and exhaustion.*

There was a group of Arabs in the desert valley, *and* their leather *water* bags had become dried up because of a drought of *no* rain.

It was a caravan stuck and exhausted in the middle of the desert, *who* had read *the signs of* their *imminent* death.

Just then Muhammad,[2] the one who gives help to both this world and the next, became visible from *the far end of* the way in order to give assistance.

He saw there a large caravan [*suffering*] upon the hot sand and a difficult and rugged route.

The tongues of their camels were hanging *out of their mouths*, and the people *were* scattered in every direction upon the sand.

The Prophet became *full of* compassion *and* said, "Listen! Some of you friends *of each other* go quickly *and* run toward those sand hills.

"*Look to see* if a black man *riding* on a camel has brought a leather *water* bag, *which* he is bringing quickly to his master.

"Bring that black camel rider to me, together with *his* camel, by the bitter command *of force if necessary.*"

Those seekers came toward the sand hills, *and* after a while they saw the very same thing *foretold by the Prophet:*

(continued on page 47)

3   The Prophet Muhammad's enemies spread the falsehood that he was crazy (meaning demon-possessed), a magician, or a poet (Q. 21:5; 52:30), capable of casting a spell on people and predicting evil calamities.

4   The Holy Qur'an refers to a bottomless pit in Hell (101:9). Muslims believe Hell to be a reality, and of different gradations that are the opposite of the ranks of blessing given to those in Paradise. There is some disagreement among scholars as to whether punishment as described in the Qur'an is eternal or endures "except as your Lord Wills" (Q. 11:108; see also 6:128).

5   In the Qur'an, the miracles initiated by the Prophets occur only by the permission of God. (See, for example, the miracles of the Prophet Jesus, Q. 3:49; 5:113.)

A slave *who was* black was traveling, like a gift giver, with a camel *and* a large leather container full of water.

Then they told him, "The Pride of Humanity *and* the Best of Men is inviting you *to come* in this direction."

He replied, "I don't know him. Who is he?" *The man* was told, "He is that sweet-natured one *with* a face *as attractive* as the *full* moon."

They made known to him the various *praiseworthy* qualities that exist *in the Prophet. The man* said, "Perhaps he is like that poet[3]

"Who made captive a group of people by means of magic *incantations.* I won't come *even* half a span toward him!"

They brought him in the direction *of the caravan*, dragging him, *while* he raised up wails and laments with ugly accusations and heated *anger.*

When they had dragged him into the presence of that cherished and honored one, *the Prophet* said, "Drink the water and also take [*more for your own water bag*]!"

He quenched the thirst of all from that leather *water* container. The camels and every person drank from that *bag of* water.

From *the man's* leather bag, he [*miraculously caused to be*] filled large leather containers and *other* bags, until the clouds of the wheeling sky were left amazed because of envy for him.

Has anyone seen *anything like* this, that the burning heat of such a deep hell[4] was made cold by means of one large leather container?

Has anyone seen *anything like* this, that leather bags such as these became full without *any* disturbance by means of one leather bag of water?

The leather bag itself was a veil, for waves of *God's* grace and favor were arriving from the Ocean of *divine* origin by the command *of the Prophet.*[5]

[*The materialists say that*] water is changed to air [*only*] by means of boiling, and that air is changed to water [*only*] by means of cold.

(*continued on page 49*)

6 God is understood in Islam to be the Causer of all causes and the Creator of all effects, in spite of the fact that to the human mind every effect appears to have a physical cause only.

7 God is depicted as expressing surprise that someone who believed only in physical causes should finally look to Him as the Originator of causes, and as suggesting that such a person would return to believing only in physical causes even if given the opportunity to return to the world.

8 The (primordial) covenant was made before the creation, between the souls of all mankind: "And when your Lord drew forth from the children of Adam, from their loins, their seed, and made them testify concerning themselves, 'Am I not Your Lord?' they said, 'But of course! We do testify!'" (Q. 7:172).

9 A Qur'anic verse tells how those who enter Hell will plead that if they were sent back to the world they would not reject the Signs of God and would be true believers. These words then follow (Q. 6:27–28). The meaning is that those who are weak in true faith in God and pure love of Truth will not be free of spiritual blindness by trying to affirm something with their minds (that is, not in their hearts) in order to avoid negative consequences.

But to the contrary: *It is God who has* brought forth the water into existence from non-existence, without *need of a physical* cause *and* beyond *the bounds of* these natural sciences.

Since, from your childhood, you have seen *physical* causes, you have clung to [*the belief that there are only physical*] causes out of ignorance.

With *your limited belief in* causes, you are oblivious and forgetful of the Causer,[6] *and so* you are tending toward *being blinded by* these veils for that *reason.*

But when *physical* causes have departed [*on the Day of Judgment*], you will beat your head *and* you will make *many cries of* "O our Lord! O our Lord!"

Then the Lord will say, "Go *back* to *physical* causes! How did you remember about My actions?[7] How amazing!"

He will reply [*to the Lord*], "After this I will see You entirely [*in all events*], I will not look at *physical causes* and the deceit [*of looking only at such*]."

God will say to him, "O you *who are* weak in repentance and *remembering* the *primordial* covenant![8] Your case is *like that in the verse,* 'If they were returned *to the world* they would surely relapse *to forbidden behavior.*'[9]

(*continued on page 51*)

10 God is "the Most Merciful of the merciful" (Q. 7:151). According to a saying of the Prophet, God said, "Truly, My Mercy prevails over My Wrath." And in another version, "My Mercy precedes My Wrath."

11 The Unperceived World is the world of the invisible, spiritual, and heavenly, from which material, sensed, and imagined things originate. In Islamic philosophy, objects in the Unperceived and physically "non-existent" world have full existence (but not everything imagined by the human mind can have existence in either world—these are regarded as "impossibles").

12 The spiritual emanation was the overflowing of the Grace, Mercy, and Bounty of God into the human heart.

13 Veils are the "covers" that prevent (most) humans from seeing the invisible causes of effects in the material world.

14 He was in an ecstatic state, full of love for God, accompanying the appearance of true faith and the knowledge of certainty of the existence of God.

15 The time for being "drowned" in ecstasy was over, and it would not benefit him to continue being immersed because it was the time for action and service to God's Will (by returning to his master, revealing the Prophet's miracle, and spreading the monotheistic faith of Islam among the people of that region).

"But I will not look at that. I will act mercifully, *since* My Mercy is full and complete; I will devote *Myself* to mercy.[10]

"I will not look at your bad agreement. *Instead* I will grant a *merciful* gift out of generosity at this moment, since you are calling *out* to Me."

The members of the caravan were astounded at *his miraculous* act *and said*, "O Muhammad! O ocean-natured one! What is this?

"You've made a small *water* bag a veil *while* you've drowned *the thirst of* both Arabs and Kurds."

About the filling of the slave's leather bag full of water from the Unperceived *World*[11] by a miracle, and making the black slave white-faced—by the permission of God Most High.

The Prophet said, "O slave, now see *that* your leather bag *is* full *of water*, so that you won't speak in complaint *about anything* good or bad."

The black man was bewildered at this demonstration *of a miracle.* His faith *in* God was appearing *like the dawn* from placelessness.

He *then* saw a fountain *which* was pouring *water* from the air and that his leather bag was a veil for the *spiritual* emanation[12] of that *fountain.*

By means of that *penetrating* vision, he also ripped through the veils,[13] so that he saw the *divinely* specified fountain of the Unperceived *World.*

In that moment his eyes filled with tears, *and* the slave became forgetful of his master and his *home* dwelling.

His arms and legs were left *drained of strength* for traveling on the way, *since* God threw a *profound* agitation into his soul.[14]

Then *the Prophet* drew him back for *his own* welfare,[15] saying, "Come to yourself! Turn back, O receiver of *divine* benefits!

"It's not the time for being amazed and bewildered. Astonishment is before you, so come on to the way *of departure, and go* promptly and quickly."

The slave placed the hands of Muhammad on *his* face *and* in the manner of a lover gave many kisses *upon them.*

(continued on page 53)

16 The Prophet Joseph is depicted as being as attractive as an angel (Q. 12:31).

17 White serves as a symbol in Rumi's poetry for a purified dervish, Sufi master, and saint who is illumined by divine knowledge and realization (sometimes depicted as one with a handsome light-skinned Turkish face). He contrasts this with an ignorant person (sometimes depicted as one with an ugly dark-skinned Hindu or Ethiopian face). These are intended as symbols of different levels of awareness of God, not as stereotypes of racial superiority or inferiority. Rumi is always concerned with inner meanings, not outward appearances, as this story shows.

18 The master is asking whether the man was born light-skinned.

19 This phrase refers to an Arabic proverb.

At that time Muhammad rubbed his blessed hand upon his face and made it happy and fortunate.

That black African and son of an Ethiopian became as white as the full moon, *and* his night changed to luminous day,

So that he became a Joseph in beauty[16] and amorous glances. *The Prophet* told him, "Now go to *your* village and speak openly *about your* situation."

He kept traveling without *awareness of* head or feet, drunk *with spiritual ecstasy.*

Then he came from the region of the caravan toward his master, riding with two full leather *water* bags.

About the master's seeing his slave *as* white,[17] his not recognizing who he was, and *his* saying, "You've killed my slave! His blood has blamed you, and God has cast you into my hands!"

The master saw him from a distance and remained confused. From bewilderment, he called the people to [*gather in the center of*] the village.

He said, "This is my large *water* skin *and* my *riding* camel. So then where has my slave with black forehead gone?

"This one coming from a distance is *like* a full moon, *so that* the light from his face strikes *blows* upon the daylight.

"Where is my slave? Perhaps he became lost, or a wolf reached him, or he was killed."

When he came in front *of him*, he asked him, "Who are you? Are you *someone* born in Yemen, or are you a Turk?[18]

"Tell *me*, what did you do to my slave? Tell the truth! If you've killed him, affirm *it and* don't seek to deceive!"

The slave answered, "Why would I have come to you if I had killed *him?* Why would I have come with my own feet into this blood?"[19]

(*continued on page 55*)

20 The lives of slaves were greatly improved following the Islamic Revelation, the only religion in which the freeing of slaves is urged in its holy scripture as an important act of charity (Q. 2:177; 90:13). The Prophet Muhammad set free all his slaves and encouraged his followers to do the same. Cruelty toward slaves could lead to damnation. People who were already Muslims could not be enslaved.

21 Rumi begins his comments here, saying that the essential soul of a saint remains after the body has died and decayed.

22 This verse expresses the classic realization of mystics in many spiritual traditions in the world: that besides the obvious reality of multiple and separate things in creation, there is also a transcendent reality of divine oneness, which is beyond separations and is like an all-encompassing Ocean within which separate things have existence.

23 Rumi refers here to intuitive and direct perception of Truth, not the indirect and speculative reasoning of the ordinary and uninspired human intellect in its efforts to understand divine revelation.

24 The saints and mystics have a different form than do the angels, but both forms are connected to divine intelligence.

25 Angels are described in the Qur'an as having three or four pairs of wings (Q. 35:1).

26 The Prophet Adam possessed an essential superiority over the angels (a completeness possessed also by the perfected prophets and saints of God). According to the Qur'an, Adam was breathed into by God of His spirit and knew "the names of all things" (interpreted by Sufis to mean the Names of God), which the angels did not know. (See Q. 15:29; 2:31–34; 7:11; 15:29; 17:61; 18:50; 20:116; 38:72.)

The master again said, "Where's my slave?" *The slave* replied, "Here am I! The hand of the Grace and Favor of God has made me bright and luminous."

The master said, "Hey, what are you talking *about?* Where's my slave? Beware! You won't escape from me except by *telling me* the truth."

The slave said, "I will tell all your hidden *doings and commands having to do* with that slave, one by one in full.

"I will tell what has happened from the time you bought me[20] until now,

"So that you may know that I am the same in *essential* existence, even though a *bright* dawn has opened up from my night-colored *body*.

"The color has become different, but the pure spirit is *completely* free from color, *the four* elements, and dust *of the body.*"

The knowers of the body quickly lose *sight* of us,[21] *but* the drinkers of spiritual water give up [*attachment to*] the leather *water* bag and jar *of the body.*

The knowers of the spirit are free from numbers *and multiplicity;*[22] they are drowned in the Ocean *that is* without "how" or "how much."

Become spirit, and know spirit by way of spirit. Become the friend of [*penetrating*] vision,[23] not the child of reasoning and supposition.

The knowers of spirit have been made connected to Intelligence, like the Angel, *but* for the sake of *Divine* Wisdom they have become two *different* forms.[24]

The Angel has received wings and feathers like a bird,[25] but this intellect *of the saints* has passed *beyond* wings[26] and has received *divine* glory and splendor.

1 "Satan threatens you with poverty and (then) orders you to (indulge in) sinful excess" (Q. 2:268).

2 Islam emphasizes the importance of avoiding certain foods viewed as unclean, such as anything dedicated or sacrificed to false gods, the meat of swine, and the meat of an animal not killed properly and mercifully.

3 Reward from God on the Day of Judgment.

4 "The unbeliever eats the food of seven stomachs" refers to those who reject the One True God and the need to practice virtue and avoid vice. (For "unbeliever," see *kāfir* in the glossary.)

5 "The (true) believer": See *mu'min* in the glossary.

6 "Mosque": Literally, "place of prostration" [*masjid*]. In Egypt, this word is pronounced "masgid." This led to the French word "mosque."

7 The Companions of the Prophet had become so filled with the Prophet's blessings and virtues that they would be true representatives of the Prophet with their guests.

7 □ The Greedy Pagan

Hear from the Qur'an[1] how Satan is terrifying you through the threat of severe poverty,

So that you might eat unclean food[2] and take unclean things out of haste *to avoid poverty, with* neither manly virtue, careful consideration, or reward[3] *from God.*

Therefore, the unbeliever eats with "seven stomachs," *and* his heart and spirit are thin and emaciated *while his* belly *is* fat.

About the coming of this saying to Muhammad—may God pour blessings and peace upon him—"The unbeliever eats the food of seven stomachs,[4] but the *true* believer[5] eats the food of a single stomach."

Some unbelievers became the guests of the Prophet. They came to the mosque[6] *at* evening time,

Saying, "O king! We've come here as travelers, O you *who are* the guest-keeper of the inhabitants of the regions *of the earth.*

"We have arrived from far away and are without food and provisions. Please scatter *your spiritual* grace and light upon our heads!"

The Prophet said, "O my Companions, divide *the guests among your-selves,* since you are full of me and my character."[7]

Each one of the Companions selected one guest. There was one obese man without equal among the guests.

(continued on page 59)

8 Alcoholic beverages are strictly forbidden in Islam, but Persian Sufi poetry is full of wine imagery, usually symbolizing spiritual states of consciousness.

9 "Father of Famine" means "famine-causing," so that there was no food left for most of the people.

10 "Ghuzz Turk" is a Turkmān of the Oghuz tribe, who were known as greedy plunderers and who invaded eastern Persia (Khorāsān) more than five hundred years after the Prophet died. Rumi here provides a vivid image of a pagan barbarian familiar to the listeners of his story.

11 "A stratagem" might have been, perhaps, tying something around his abdomen to ease the pain so he could sleep.

12 He desired to be where he could relieve himself, and this mental image developed into a dream.

13 A place in the open, where there were no people around.

He had a huge and bulky body, *and* no one took him *home*. He remained in the mosque, *neglected* like dregs in the *wine* cup.[8]

Since he remained *unselected* by all, Muhammad took him *as his guest*. There were seven milk-producing goats in the flock *belonging to the Prophet*.

Though the goats would reside at the *Prophet's* house in order to be milked at meal times,

That "Father of Famine"[9] *and* son of a Ghuzz Turk[10] ate *all* the bread and soup *in the house* and *all* the milk of each of the seven goats.

All the members of the house became disturbed with anger, because everyone was desirous of the goat milk.

He alone ate the portions of eighteen persons *and* made his free-loading belly *as stout* as a drum.

He left at time for sleeping and sat in his small room. Then the servant girl shut *his* door from rage.

She cast a door chain from the outside *to lock him in*, since she was full of anger and disturbed because of him.

When the pagan man was *in an* urgent *state* and *suffering from* bellyache in the middle of the night or dawn,

He hurried from his *sleeping* carpet toward the door, *but* he found the door *bound* shut when he put his hand on the door.

That maker of clever tricks used different kinds of strategies to open the door, but those fetters didn't loosen.

His urgency became more demanding, *and* the room was cramped. He remained confused, without remedy, and stupefied.

He used a stratagem[11] and slid back to sleep. In a dream, he saw himself in a ruined place.

Because [*the image of*] a ruined place[12] was in his mind, the object of his sight was in that same *kind of* place in *his* dream.

When he saw himself in an empty desolate place,[13] he *was in* such need *that* at that moment he defecated.

(continued on page 61)

14 This verse refers to how the wrongdoing rejectors of the One God who are in Hell will beg for "destruction" (Q. 25:14) or complete death and annihilation, but they will continue to exist and suffer. (See *kāfir* in the glossary.)

15 He had lost the way to spiritual salvation.

16 A phrase from the Qur'an (2:138), it refers to a dyeing vat for coloring clothes. Divine Mercy covers up sins with a different "color." Rumi here uses the term in a similar way: covering up from being seen.

He *then* awoke and saw that his bedclothes were full of excrement *and* he became crazed from anguish and agitation.

A hundred loud cries arose from within him because of such a public disgrace not covered *up* by earth.

He said, "My sleep *is* worse than my wakefulness, since I eat *on* this side and I defecate on that side."

He was crying out, "What ruin! What destruction!"—just like an unbeliever[14] in the bottom of *his* tomb,

Waiting, *and* saying, "When will this night *come* to an end?"—so that the sound might come forth of the door in being opened,

In order that he might escape, like an arrow from the bow, so that no one might see him *in* such *a situation* as this.

The story is lengthy, *so* I am making it short. That door was opened, *and* he was freed from suffering and sorrow.

About the opening of the door by Muhammad—peace be upon him—for the guest, and making himself hidden so that he might not see the image of the opener *and so that* he might not be ashamed and might go out *of the room* with bold *confidence*.

Muhammad came at dawn and opened the door. He offered the Way to that one *who had* lost the way.[15]

Muhammad opened the door and *quickly* became hidden, so that the unfortunate man might not become embarrassed,

So that he might come out and go with bold *confidence, and* so that he might not see the back or face of the door opener.

Either he was hidden behind something, or the veil of God hid him from him.

For "the hue of God"[16] sometimes makes *something* hidden *and* winds an incomparable veil over the one looking,

So that he may not notice the enemy next to him. *And* the Power of God is more than that, *much* more.

(continued on page 63)

17 This idiom means to end up in a miserable state because of foolish and careless actions.

18 This line may refer to a verse in the Qur'an, "And it may be that you hate a thing, and (yet) it is a something good for you" (2:216).

19 This title of the Prophet is based on a verse of the Qur'an in which God addressed Muhammad: "And We did not send you except as a mercy to (all) peoples" (21:107).

20 That is, the work was not suitable for a Prophet of God to do.

21 "By your life" refers to how honored the Prophet Muhammad was when spoken to by God (at the beginning of a verse) in the form of an oath: "Truly, by your life (O Muhammad)" (Q. 15:72).

22 "Representative [khalīfa]": God made Adam his representative, or vice-regent, on earth (Q. 2:30) and thereby all the Prophets sent by God to mankind. Spiritually, the Muslim saints are also representatives of God and the Prophet. Politically, the head of the Islamic state was called the Caliph and, in this sense, was the Prophet's successor.

23 There is a hidden wisdom involved of which the people of the Prophet's household had no knowledge.

Muhammad was seeing *all* the conditions of the *previous* night *which occurred* for *the guest,* but the command of the Lord prevented him *from acts of rescue,*

Such as to open a way *for the guest to escape* before the mistake *was made* so that *the guest* might not fall into a well[17] because of that shameful act.

But it was the Wisdom *of God* and the Command of Heaven that he should find himself *in* such *an embarrassing situation* as that.

There are many *kinds of* antagonism which are friendship[18] *in reality, and there are* many *types of* destruction which are constructive *in reality.*

Then an interfering meddler deliberately brought the bedclothes, *which were* full of filth, to the Prophet,

Saying, "See *how* your guest has done such as this!" *The Prophet who is* "a mercy to *all* peoples"[19] smiled in a certain way,

Saying, "Bring that jug *of water* here before *me,* so that I may wash everything with my own hands."

Everyone leaped up, saying, "For the sake of God *please don't!* Our souls and bodies are *all* sacrificed for you.

"Please desist *and* let us wash this filth! This manner *of task* is the job for hands, not the work of the heart.[20]

"O you who are called 'By your life,'[21] God said *the word* 'life' in regard to you. *And* then he made *you His* representative[22] and seated *you* upon a throne *of dominion.*

"We are living for the sake of serving you. Since you are doing *this act of* service, then who are we?"

The Prophet said, "I know that, but this is *an unusual* moment, since there is a *divine* wisdom[23] for me *to be involved* in this washing."

They were waiting, saying, "This is the word of a Prophet, [*so let's wait*] until it becomes clear what these secrets are."

The Prophet was washing those soiled things in earnest, specifically because of the command of God—not *because of* imitation or pretense [*by trying to appear spiritual*].

(continued on page 65)

24 He did not act out of pretense, as in the verse referring to the Prophet, "His heart did not falsify what he saw" (Q. 53:11). The heart is traditionally viewed as the source of deep thinking.

25 The amulet perhaps had a magic pattern or the image of a deity believed capable of warding off danger.

26 "Hand of God" refers to the pledge of allegiance made to the Prophet by his followers, who took his hand, when, as the Qur'an says, "the Hand of God is over their hands" (48:10). Sufi masters also recite this verse when accepting allegiance from new disciples.

27 In other words, "May he be protected from evil influences." This is the ancient belief that sickness, misfortune, and death may be caused by someone's envious and hateful gaze.

28 This is the ancient custom of rending garments during intense grief or joy. In Islamic cultures, men might tear their shirts at the collar or tear an outer garment, since public nudity is forbidden.

29 Here (as in Q. 5:95), the meaning is "beware of evil."

Since *his* heart was saying to him, "Wash these, for there is much wisdom in this situation."[24]

About **the cause of the returning of the guest to the house of Muhammad—may peace be upon him—at the moment when Muhammad was washing his soiled sleeping carpet with his own hands.** *And about* **his becoming embarrassed, tearing his robe, his lamenting for himself and for his** *loss of* **happiness.**

That base pagan had an amulet[25] as a memorial. He saw *that* it *was* lost, and he became restless and uneasy.

He said *to himself,* "I must have unknowingly left the amulet there, *in* the small room where I had a place *last* night."

Although he was ashamed, greed carried *off* his shame. Greed is a dragon; it's not a small thing.

For the sake of the amulet, he ran quickly into Muhammad's house and saw him.

That "Hand of God"[26] was cheerfully washing that filth by himself—*may* the evil eye *be* far *from* him![27]

Concern for the amulet went from his mind, an agitation manifested within him, and he tore the upper part of *his* shirt.[28]

He kept hitting *his* face and head *with his* two hands *and* was pounding *the top of his* head upon the wall and door,

In such a manner that blood was flowing from his nose and head. And that great lord, *the Prophet,* felt compassion for him.

The guest was shouting, *and* the people gathered near him. The pagan was saying, "O people, beware!"[29]

He was pounding upon *his* head, saying, "O head lacking understanding!" *And* he was hitting upon *his* chest, saying, "O chest lacking light!"

(continued on page 67)

30 Rumi uses philosophical terms: the "universal," or whole, and the "particular," or part. The pagan prostrated his face upon the ground, which he compared to the Prophet's greatness.

31 Fear or awe of God is nowadays much misunderstood. However, it is an essential virtue related to love, which involves a cautiousness or dread of doing anything to cause distance between the worshiper and the Creator, who is the Source of all love, beauty, wisdom, compassion, protection, salvation, and so on.

32 "Prayer-direction [*qibla*]": A marker that indicates the direction of prayer facing Mecca, and specifically the Ka'ba (see the glossary). The word has to do with praying to God "face to face."

33 He opened the "eye of the heart" so that the man was able to see the spiritual realities of things and situations.

34 That is, God, the Provider of all nourishment.

35 This is a quote in Arabic from the Qur'an (9:82). It means that those who weep in neediness toward God will laugh with joy in the Hereafter, but worldly people who laugh for the sake of worldly comfort and selfish pursuits will weep. Rumi presents one of his major teachings: that God gives to His creatures to the extent of their need. As he says elsewhere, "So increase (your) need at once, O needy one, so that the Sea of Generosity may surge forth in Benevolence."

36 That is, combine weeping with constant ardent faith in God in your prayers.

He was prostrating *and* saying, "O *you who are like* the whole earth, this contemptible part[30] is ashamed because of you [*and your greatness*].

"You, who are the whole, are humble *in submission* to His Command. *But* I, who am a part, am a barbarous tyrant, evil and led astray.

"You, who are the whole, are servile and trembling because of *awe of* God.[31] *But* I, who am a part, am *involved* in rebellion and trying to surpass *God.*"

He was raising *his* face to the sky *in* every moment, saying, "O prayer-direction[32] of the world! I don't have a face *to face you.*"

When he was trembling *of limbs* and throbbing *of heart* beyond bounds, Muhammad drew him into his embrace.

He made him *to be* quiet, soothed him abundantly, and gave him *spiritual* understanding.[33]

As long as the cloud doesn't weep, the meadow won't smile. *And as long as the infant doesn't weep, the milk won't flow from the mother's breasts.*

The baby *whose life is only that* of a single day *intuitively* knows the way *to get milk,* thinking, "I will cry until the kind nurse arrives."

Don't you know that the Nurse of *all* nurses[34] doesn't give milk freely without *your* weeping?

God said, "Let them weep greatly."[35] Keep *your* ear [*and listen to these words*] so that the Grace of the Creator may pour "milk."

The weeping of the cloud and the burning of the sun are the column *upholding* the world; *in* the same way, you should twist both *of these* cords *together.*[36]

(continued on page 69)

37 Rumi uses the philosophical terms "accidents" (external qualities that happen to occur) and "substance" (the underlying nature, or body).

38 This continues the metaphor of the infant receiving sweet milk, and here means the nourishment of the creation in general.

39 Refers to a verse in the Qur'an (73:20) about spending money and property in the cause of God—a form of self-denial that Rumi interprets here as doing (moderately) ascetic practices, which are richly rewarded spiritually.

40 This is the Prophet's explanation of a verse in the Qur'an (32:17): "God says, 'I have prepared for My righteous servants that which no eye has seen and no ear has heard, and which the heart of man cannot conceive.'" This is similar to a verse in the biblical New Testament (Corinthians 2:9, based on Isaiah 64:3 and Jeremiah 3:16).

41 "Pearls" are the spiritual benefits of voluntary fasting, combined with intensive remembrance of God [*dhikru 'llāh*].

42 A verse in the Qur'an reads, "Certainly, God wishes to take away uncleanliness from you, (O) members of the (Prophet's) house, and (then) He will purify you completely" (33:33).

43 This refers to Rumi's practice of elaborating his stories in the *Mathnawi* with associations of related topics of wisdom and substories before returning to the main story.

44 He was going into a deep state of spiritual drunkenness in which he would be unable to function rationally and soberly in order to accept true worship of God through Islam.

For if there were no burning of the sun and tears of the cloud, there would never be *any* thick and full body or external qualities.[37]

Each of the four seasons would never be abundant if this heat and weeping were not the origin.

Since the burning of the sun and the weeping of the world's clouds continue to keep the world sweet of mouth,[38]

So keep the sun of *your* intelligence burning *and* keep your eyes shining with tears like the clouds.

Give a loan[39] *to God and* reduce *the quantity* of the food *you eat* for your body, so that the face of "what no eye has seen"[40] may appear.

When the body makes itself empty of excrement, God makes *it* full of musk and the most magnificent pearls.[41]

Someone gives up being filled of this foulness, and he takes purity in exchange. His body *then* consumes the "fruits" of *the verse* "He will purify you."[42]

About the soothing by Muhammad—peace be upon him—of that Arab guest, giving him quietness following *his* agitation, weeping, and lamenting for himself which he was doing in embarrassment, regret, and the fire of hopelessness.

This speech has no end.[43] The Arab *guest* remained in *a state of* wonder because of the kindnesses of that *spiritual* king.

He [*felt that he*] wanted to become crazy,[44] *and* his mind fled, *but* the hand of Muhammad's intelligence drew him back.

He said, "Come to this side!" *The guest* came in such a manner as a person rises up from a heavy *state of* sleep.

He said, "Come *in* this direction! Don't [*lose your mind*]! Take care, *and* come to yourself! For there are *important* actions *having to do* with you from this side."

(*continued on page 71*)

45   The Testimony (of Faith) is the "bearing witness" [*shahādat*], which is said in the presence of Muslim witnesses when someone accepts the truth of the Islamic Revelation and converts to Islam. The testimony is said in Arabic: "I bear witness that there is no divinity except (the One) God. And I bear witness that Muhammad is His slave and His messenger."

46   He will leave behind worldly existence, where consuming much leads to shame and regret, and will enter spiritual reality, where abstaining much leads to spiritual joy and fulfillment.

47   He refers to the Middle Eastern custom of eating on the floor or the ground with the food placed upon a cloth, or occasionally upon leather. Here, the reference is to a tablecloth of endless spiritual blessings.

He splashed water upon his face, *and the guest* came into *a state of being able* to speak *again*, saying, "O Witness of God, present *me with the words of* the Testimony *of Faith*,[45]

"So that I may give witness *to the truth* and go out of *my state of unbelief*, *for* I am fed up with *worldly* existence, and I will go into that wilderness."[46]

About the offering by Muhammad—may the peace *of God* be upon him—of the Testimony *of Faith* to his guest.

This speech has no end. Muhammad presented the *Testimony of* Faith and that young man accepted *it*—

That Testimony which has *always* been *the source of* happiness and good fortune and has released the bound shackles *of unbelief*.

He became a *true believer.* Muhammad *then* told him, "Be my guest tonight as well!"

The guest said, "By God! I am your guest forever, whatever place I am, *and* to whatever place that I go.

"I have been made alive and liberated *from slavery* by you, and *I am* your gate keeper in this world and the next, *always dining* at your table-cloth."[47]

The Arab became the guest of the Prophet that night. He drank *only* half the milk of one goat and shut his lips.

The Prophet pressed him, *saying*, "Drink *more* milk and *eat* the thin loaves *of bread*." *The guest* replied, "By God, I've become full—without *any* pretense.

"This is not *said from* insincerity, *concern for* reputation, or deceit, *since* I've become more full than *from* what *I ate* last night."

(continued on page 73)

48 See *Īmān* in the glossary.

49 This refers to the story in the Qur'an of the mother of Jesus, who was driven by the pain of childbirth toward a palm tree and heard a voice from Heaven telling her not to grieve, since there was a source of water beneath her to drink, and a palm tree to shake that would provide fruit for her to eat (19:22–25). Mary is venerated by Muslims. According to the Qur'an, she was addressed by an angel: "O Mary! Truly, God has selected and purified you and chosen you from above (all) the women of the world" (Q. 3:42).

50 The Qur'an contains the frightful image of Hell as very greedy to consume more of the souls of wrongdoers on the Day of Judgment: "(On the) Day We will ask Hell, 'Are you filled?' And it will say, '[No], are there (any) more?'" (Q. 50:30).

All of the people *living in* the house *of the Prophet* remained in *a state of* amazement, *thinking*, "How did this lamp became full from *only* this one drop of olive oil?"

And *"How did* the stomach of such an elephant become filled by that which is *a small portion of* food for a bird?"

Whispering occurred among the men and women, saying, "That *man with the* body of an elephant is eating the amount of a gnat!"

The greed and false opinions of unbelief became *thrown* down, *and* the dragon became satisfied with the *portion of* food *suitable* for an ant.

The greedy beggar's viewpoint of unbelief went from him, *and* the morsel of *true* Faith[48] made him thick and stout [*of spirit*].

The one who was trembling from a sickness of hunger saw the fruit of Paradise, like Mary.[49]

The sight of the fruit of Paradise rushed to his eyes, *and* his stomach, *as ravenous* as Hell,[50] obtained rest.

O you *who have* made *yourself* content with the Faith by words *only!* The substance of *true* Faith is a great blessing and a delicious food [*for the soul*].

1 The preceding story in the *Mathnawi* is about a man who foolishly made a bear his companion, would not heed advice, became more stubborn, and died disastrously.

2 That is, give advice.

3 The Prophet had frowned and turned away from a poor blind man who had interrupted his conversation with pagan chieftains in Mecca by saying, "O Prophet of God, teach me what God has taught you." God sent a revelation (Q. 80:1–10) to the Prophet that criticized him because the man had come with awe of God and was striving sincerely for the truth. This man became a Muslim, and in later years the Prophet would greet him humbly, saying, "Welcome to the one regarding whom my Lord rebuked me."

4 Rumi portrays God's speech to Muhammad, an elaboration of the shorter account in the Qur'an.

5 "Basra" and "Tabūk" together mean "far distant places." Basra, the port city at the mouth of the Tigris River in 'Irāq, was not actually founded until just after the Prophet's death. Tabūk was a town to which Muhammad led an army to face a reported Byzantine threat.

6 The Prophet said, "Men are (like) mines: if you can understand, you will know their choice of pagan polytheism or their choice of Islam."

8 □ The Blind One

When your *attempted* remedy increases the suffering[1] *of the one you try to help*, then *turn from him and* tell *your* story[2] to a seeker *of truth and* recite *the chapter in the Qur'an entitled* "He Frowned."[3]

Since the blind man had come as a seeker of truth, it is not suitable to wound his heart because of his poverty.

"You are desirous[4] for the right guidance of *pagan* chieftains, so that the common people may learn *the right way* from *their* leaders.

"O Muhammad, you saw that some of the ruling chiefs *of Mecca* were listening *to you, so* you became pleased and happy that perhaps

"These chiefs may become good friends of the Religion *of Islam, since* these are heads over *tribes* of Arabs and Ethiopians.

"*And that perhaps* the fame *of this* may pass through Basra and Tabūk,[5] since 'The people *follow* after the religion of *their* kings.'

"Because of this, you turned *away your* face from the rightly guided blind man, and you became annoyed,

"Telling *him,* 'This relaxed situation [*with opponents*] seldom occurs in an opportunity *such* as this—*but* you are among *my* friends and companions, and your time [*to talk with me*] is plentiful.

"'You are pressing upon me *with your needs* during a limited moment. So I'm giving you this advice, *but* not because of anger or quarrelling.'

"O Muhammad! In the presence of God, this one blind man is better than a hundred emperors and prime ministers.

"Beware, and bring to mind *the saying* 'Men are mines,'[6] *and so* a particular mine is of greater *value* than a hundred thousand *others*.

(*continued on page 77*)

7 A major theme of Rumi is that the lover must feel the pain of separation from the beloved (a symbol for God)—a pain of yearning that has a sweet pleasure because it brings to mind the beauty of the one longed for.

8 This verse refers to the ongoing revelation of the Qur'an to Muhammad.

9 "Nourishment from a sun" means benefit from sunlight. Bats were assumed (incorrectly) to be blind and to dislike sunlight.

10 The dung beetle, or scarab, feeds on animal dung, which it pushes into little balls. It was viewed as becoming faint and dying from perfume, but revived by the smell of dung.

11 A touchstone is a kind of stone that demonstrates the presence of real gold by changing color when rubbed against it. The touchstone was used for centuries by assayers as a test for genuine gold.

"The mine *full* of hiding rubies and agates is better than a hundred thousand mines of copper.

"O Muhammad! Wealth has no advantage in this [*situation*]. *Rather,* a heart is needed *which is* full of love and pain and sadness[7] [*from yearning*].

"A blind man of luminous heart has come. Do not close the door, *but* offer him advice, since *spiritual* advice is his right.

"If two or three stupid fools have denied and rejected you [*as a Prophet*], you should not be sour, since you are a mine of sugar.

"If a few fools *try to* fix a slanderous accusation upon you, God continues to give witness for your sake."[8]

Muhammad said, "I am free from caring about the world's acceptance *of me.* There is no worry for the one whose witness is God.

"If a bat has any nourishment from a sun,[9] that is proof that it is not the *real* sun. So the hatred of 'bats' is proof that I am the radiant glorious sun.

"If the dung beetle[10] prefers some rose water, that proves *it's* not *real* rose water.

"If a counterfeit coin is the *willing* customer for the touchstone,[11] [*the response of*] defect and doubt comes into the touchstone concerning it.

"Know this: the robber desires night, not day. I am not night, *but* I am day, since I am shining into the world."

1 | "The friend of God" is a Muslim Sufi, or dervish.

2 | God spoke severe and soothing words, giving both warning and reassurance.

3 | "Revelation" means verses of the Qur'an that were revealed after the believers left the Prophet's mosque in the middle of his sermon at hearing of the arrival of a long-awaited caravan from Syria. "But if they see a (possible) bargain or a (temporary) diversion, they scatter toward it and leave you (O Muhammad) standing. Say: 'What (ever) is in the presence of God is better than a (worldly) amusement or bargain. And God is the best of providers'" (62:11).

4 | Muslims attend a special congregational prayer on Friday afternoons, which lasts for an hour or two. Muslims are free to engage in business before and after the prayer (unlike the Jewish Sabbath). The service consists of a sermon followed by congregational prayer. As a result of the above-mentioned verse of the Qur'an, worshipers are not supposed to leave the mosque before the sermon and ritual prayer are finished.

9 □ The Arrival of the Caravan

Whatever may hurl you apart from the friend of God,[1] don't listen to it, since it has loss upon loss for you.

Don't take it, even though the profit may be a hundred times a hundred. Don't separate from the poor dervish who is the treasurer of divine blessings for the sake of gold!

Listen to this: how much pain God caused the Companions of the Prophet when He spoke hot and cool[2] words of Revelation.[3]

Since, at the sound of the drum announcing the arrival of a caravan during a year of economic distress, they made the *Friday congregational prayer*[4] useless to them without hesitation,

Thinking, "Since others must not be able to buy cheap and take away from us the profit of that merchandise driven from afar by camels."

As a result, the Prophet remained alone during the congregational prayer, together with only two or three poor men who were firm in faith and full of neediness [*for God's Mercy*].

God said in Revelation, "How did the sound of the drum, worldly amusements, and the lure of commerce separate you from a man of God?

"Certainly, you scattered and rushed after wheat with crazed passion. Then you left a Prophet standing [*during the sacred assembly before God*].

"For the sake of wheat, you sowed the seeds of futility and abandoned that Messenger of God.

"His company is better than worldly diversions and wealth. Look: whom have you abandoned? Rub your eyes!

(*continued on page 81*)

5   This phrase is quoted from the Qur'an (5:117).

"But, in regard to your greed, has it not become certain that I am the Provider and 'the best of providers'?"5

The One who gives an allotment from Himself to wheat will never let your trusts and reliances upon Him to be lost.

Yet, for the sake of wheat, you have become separated from Him who caused the wheat to be sent from Heaven.

1 This verse refers to the primordial covenant made between God and the souls of all humanity: "And when your Lord drew forth from the children of Adam, from their loins, their seed, and made them testify concerning themselves, 'Am I not your Sustaining Lord?' they said, 'But of course! We do testify!'" (Q. 7:172). A major goal of Muslim mystics, or Sufis, has been to "remember" this state of awareness and commitment to the Creator that has been forgotten by nearly all of humanity. Another meaning of this verse is that love for God has always existed within the human soul.

2 The Prophet had leaned against one of the palm trunks holding up the roof of the mosque during his weekly sermon on Friday (the day for required congregational prayers in Islam) in Medina, Arabia. After the Prophet mounted a newly constructed pulpit with stairs, it is said that the palm trunk made a lamenting sound and split. The Prophet hugged it, and its groaning gradually stopped.

3 The anguished longing of separation of the lover from the Beloved is a major theme in Rumi's poetry, and he often uses the metaphor of the groaning pillar's longing love for the Prophet.

10 □ The Groaning Pillar

The call of "Am I not"[1] *your Lord?* continues to come from Him every moment, *and* essential and outward qualities *of things* are becoming existent.

Although *the reply of* "But of course!" isn't coming from them, yet their arrival *into physical existence* from the non-existent *realm* is *itself a reply of* "Yes, of course!"

Listen to a story, without delay, concerning what I have said in explanation about the awareness of wood and stone.

Concerning the lamentation of the groaning pillar when they constructed a pulpit[2] for the Prophet—may God pour blessings and peace upon him. *This was* because the congregation had become large, and they said, "We can't see your blessed face at the time of *your* preaching." And *about* the hearing of that *pillar's* complaint by the Prophet and his Companions, and the clear questions and answers *exchanged by* Muhammad—may the blessings and peace of God be upon him—with the pillar.

The groaning pillar was lamenting about its separation[3] from the Prophet, like someone possessed of intelligence.

The Prophet said, "What do you desire, O pillar?" It said, "My soul has become [*like a wound full of*] blood because of separation from you.

"I was your support, *but* you rushed away from me, *and* you made a place to lean *against* on top of the pulpit."

The Prophet said, "Do you wish to be made *into* a palm tree so that anyone from the east or west may pick *date* fruit from you?

(continued on page 85)

4 In other words, "Don't have less desire than a piece of wood has in longing to return home to the direct presence of God."

5 All Muslims believe (as do Christians and many Jews) in the Resurrection of the Dead, followed by the Day of Judgment, when wrongdoing will receive equivalent punishment, virtuous acts will receive many times the equivalent reward, and God will forgive anyone He chooses.

6 The saint and mystic who is divinely "attracted" spends most of the day involved in worship of God and companionship with other lovers of God.

7 "The seven heavens and the earth and (all) that is therein glorify Him, and there is not a thing but celebrates His praise, but you do not understand their praise" (Q. 27:43). "Have you not seen that whatever is in the Heavens and the earth glorifies God, and the birds as they spread their wings? Every one (of them) knows its prayer and its glorification, and God is the Knower of what they do" (Q. 24:41). Elsewhere, Rumi says, "The (skeptical) philosopher who is a disbelieving rejector toward the (miracle of the pillar which was) groaning is estranged from [the knowledge gained by] the (spiritual) senses of the saints." And also: "For you, the (groaning) pillar of the mosque is something dead, (but) in the presence of Muhammad, it is a lover (whose) heart (is) carried away."

"Or *do you wish that* God may make you a *lofty* cypress tree in the world *to come,* so that you will remain fresh and new for eternity?"

It said, "I wish for that which became enduring *because of* its permanence." O unaware one, listen! Don't be less than a piece of wood![4]

The Prophet buried the pillar in the ground, so that it may become resurrected like mankind *on* the Day of Judgment,[5]

So that you may know that everyone whom God has called [*and chosen for Himself*] remains inactive from all the labor of *this* world.

Since anyone whose work and burden is from God[6] has found entry *in* that place [*in the Hereafter*] and goes beyond *the need for worldly* work.

But as for the one who has *received* no gift concerning *divine* secrets, he will never confirm as true the outcry of inanimate things.[7]

1 Here, Muhammad is praised by the use of plays on words for "salt" that also mean handsome, elegant, and tasteful.

2 The [Hadīth] reports that describe the pious actions of the Prophet.

3 Muhammad's spiritual heirs are the Muslim saints, mystics, and Sufi masters who combine knowledge about Islam, faithfulness to the model of the pious life of the Prophet, and God-given spiritual insight and realization.

4 The spiritual heir of Muhammad is with you as a spiritual presence, but you can perceive this presence only through the "spiritual senses" of your soul.

5 Rumi advises using spiritual insight and perception to recognize the spiritual descendants of Muhammad.

6 "The pure Light of the King" refers to the Light of God as well as the spiritual light of Muhammad and his spiritual heirs, the Sufi saints and masters.

7 The essential identity of man is spirit, which is beyond spatial dimensions.

8 That is, until death, when divine realities will be unveiled to the soul.

9 "The rain of the Lord": The reviving inspiration of spiritual knowledge and love that is hidden in the present moment, to which Sufi mystics seek attunement.

11 □ 'Āyisha

Regarding the *spiritual* "salt"[1] by which Muhammad is more handsome *than others,* he is more eloquent than the *most elegant* "seasoned" account *about him.*[2]

And this *spiritual* "salt" remains by means of his heritage. Those *spiritual* heirs of his[3] are with you, *so* look for them!

He is seated in before you,[4] but where do you have a "front"? He is in front of you, *but* where is the soul that thinks about "front"?

If you think you have a "front" and "back," you are bound to the body and excluded from [*contact with*] the soul.

For "below," "above," "front," and "back" are qualities of the body. *But* the essence of the shining soul is beyond *physical* directions *and dimensions.*

Open up *your spiritual* vision[5] by means of the pure Light of the King,[6] so that you won't imagine *things* like a near-sighted person,

And *think* that you are only this *body* in *states of* sorrow and happiness, and nothing else. O *you who are essentially a* non-existent one![7] *Where is the relevance of* "front" and "back" for non-existence?

It is a day of rain, *so* travel on until evening[8]—not *going* through this *physical* rain, *but* by the rain of the Lord.[9]

The story of the questioning by 'Āyisha—may God be pleased with her—of Muhammad—may God pour blessings and peace upon him—saying, "The rain was falling today. Since you went to the graveyard, how are your clothes not wet?"

(continued on page 89)

10 'Āyisha was the daughter of Muhammad's closest disciple, Abu Bakr, who was given the title of "The Pious Witness to the Truth" [*Siddīq*] and who gave his daughter, 'Āyisha, in marriage to the Prophet when she was a girl (a marriage not consummated until her adolescence). 'Āyisha was Muhammad's favorite wife, honored by the feminine form of her father's title, *Siddīqa*, and she transmitted many accounts and sayings of the Prophet.

11 The Prophet Muhammad wore a turban, or head-wrap, over his head as an expression of piety. Prior to Islam, it was a centuries-old tradition for Christians and Jews to cover their heads in prayer, and all day as a reminder to be constantly in a state of prayer.

12 A woman's head-covering also expresses piety. The Qur'an ordered veiling of the face only for the Prophet's wives, to protect them from being harassed by enemies (Q. 33:59). Otherwise, the Qur'an states that Muslim women should dress modestly, interpreted to mean the covering of head, arms, and legs (Q. 24:31). Veiling of all or most of the face is a custom and an ancient pre-Islamic practice in some Muslim cultures and is not a requirement of the religion.

13 The cause of spiritual blessings was contact with a garment worn by the Prophet.

14 The rain indicates unseen influences coming from the "upper Heaven," conceived as seven or more spherical layers and "skies," which are more spiritual in proximity to the limits of the creation at the "Divine Throne" (the unveiled Presence of God).

15 The "justice of (Divine) Grandeur" means influences expressing the divine attributes of warning, admonishment, severity, and just punishment, which are in contrast to influences expressing divine forgiveness, mercy, and kindness.

Muhammad went to the graveyard one day. He went *along* with the bier *which carried the corpse* of a man among *his* companions.

∾

When the Prophet came back from the graveyard, he went to the pious lady ['Āyisha]¹⁰ and [*soon*] shared secrets *with her.*

When the eyes of *that* truthful lady glanced upon his face, she came before him and placed her hand on him,

And on his turban¹¹ and face and his hair, on the *front of his* collar and his chest and arms.

The Prophet said, "What are you looking for *in such a* rush?" She said, "It rained from the clouds today.

"I'm in search, seeking *for something on* your clothes, *but* I'm not finding *any* moisture from the rain. Oh, how amazing!"

The Prophet said, "What cloth *covering* have you thrown over your head?" She said, "I made that cloak of yours a *woman's veil*."¹²

He said, "It is for that *reason,*¹³ O pure-hearted one, *that* God revealed the unperceived *Heavenly* rain¹⁴ to your pure eyes.

"That rain is not from these clouds of yours—*since* there are other clouds and different skies."

∾

About the questioning by the pious lady ['Āyisha]—may God be pleased with her—of Muhammad—may God pour blessings and peace upon him, saying, "What was the secret of today's rain?"

The truthful lady ['Āyisha] said, "O *you who are the* best part of *created* existence! What was the *hidden* wisdom of today's rain?

"Was this *one of* the rains of *Divine* Mercy, or is it for the sake of the warning and justice of *Divine* Grandeur?¹⁵

"Was it from the gentleness of the qualities of Spring, or from the qualities of Autumn *so* full of misfortune and hardship?"

(continued on page 91)

16 According to the Qur'an, God created two parallel races on earth to worship Him (Q. 51:56): mankind and the jinn ("genies"). The latter are usually invisible to humans but can take any form they like; some are pious believers in God, others mischievous, and some evil.

17 Greedy desires are necessary to maintain worldly existence and survival.

18 Rumi interprets, in this section, a saying of the Prophet Muhammad, "If not for the foolishness (of the people) the world would be destroyed." Rumi says elsewhere, in regard to greedy kings, that "God placed a seal upon their eyes and mouths for the sake of the stability of (the affairs of) the world, so that throne and crown may (continue to) be sweet to them." Without such forgetfulness of God, human beings would be too immersed in ecstatic worship to feed and clothe themselves, farm, buy and sell, and maintain civilization.

19 All distinctions between virtues and faults would disappear if the full light of Truth were to shine upon this world. Therefore, God maintains a balance by means of "heavenly rain."

The Prophet said, "This rain is for the sake of soothing the sorrows which are caused by the afflictions that are upon the race of Adam.[16]

"For if mankind were to remain upon that fire of misery, much destruction and loss would occur.

"This world would be devastated at that time, and all greedy desires would depart[17] from humanity."

Heedless disregard of God is the pillar supporting this world,[18] O dear one. [And too much] consciousness of God is a calamity for this world.

Intelligent awareness is derived from that Heavenly world, and when it becomes dominant, this world becomes humbled and destroyed.

Intelligent awareness of God is like the sun, and greed is like ice; intelligent awareness is like the water, and this world is like the dirt.

A little "sprinkling" of that awareness keeps arriving from that Heavenly world, so that greed and envy may not growl and roar too loudly in this world.

But if the "sprinkling" coming from the Unperceived world becomes greater, no virtues or faults would remain in this world.[19]

1 Zayd was a freed slave and adopted son of the Prophet, who told him that he spent his nights in prayer and his days in thirst until he became able to see the people in Paradise and those in Hell. The Prophet told him to keep this knowledge secret: "You have realized (something), so hold it tight." Rumi elaborates on this story.

2 In transcendent unitive consciousness, nothing in the creation is separate from anything else, including different religions and various divine revelations, because everything reflects the divine unity.

3 He refers to "beginninglessness," the eternity before the beginning of time and the creation of the universe, and "endlessness," the eternity following the end of time.

4 It was customary for a traveler to bring home gifts from his travels.

5 The Seven Hells are mentioned in the Qur'an (15:43-44).

12 □ Zayd

About the Prophet's asking—may God bless him and give *him* peace—of Zayd, "How are you this morning, and how did you *feel when you* rose *from sleep?"* And his reply, saying, "O Messenger of God, this morning I am a *true* believer."[1]

The Prophet said to Zayd one morning, "How are you this morning, O good-*hearted* friend?"

Zayd answered, "A faithful servant *of God.*" He asked him again, "Where is the sign from the garden of Faith, if it has blossomed?"

Zayd replied, "I've been thirsty *during* the days, *and* I haven't slept at night because of love and the burnings *in my heart*—

"To such an extent that I've passed through the days and nights in the same way that the tip of a spear passes through a shield.

"For from that side, all religions are one,[2] and a hundred thousand years and a single hour are one.

"Pre-eternity and post-eternity are united.[3] The intellect has no way to that side by means of search and investigation."

The Prophet said, "Where is a gift brought *home* from this road[4] *which you traveled?* Bring *it forth!—something* suitable for the understanding and intellects of these regions."

Zayd replied, "When people are looking at the sky, I see the Throne *of God,* together with those *in the area* of the Throne.

"The eight Paradises *and* the Seven Hells[5] are visible in front of me, just like the idol in front of the idolater.

(continued on page 95)

6 Zayd can foresee those destined to go to Paradise or Hell.

7 "(On) the Day (of Judgment) when (some) faces will turn white (with joy) and (some) faces will turn black (with gloom)" (Q. 3:106–107). Here, "white" and "black" are symbolic of light, purity, and virtue, versus darkness, sin, and misery. In Arabic grammar, a man is called white to mean that he is free from moral defects.

8 That is, known to the (most advanced) Sufis.

9 He means before deeds become visible on the Day of Judgment.

10 A saying of the Prophet begins, "The fortunate and blessed person was (decreed to be) fortunate in his mother's womb."

11 "The wrongdoers will be known by their marks" (Q. 55:41). See also, "some will be miserable" (Q. 11:105).

12 That is, those who are in the intermediate state between death and the Resurrection.

13 "Anatolians" literally means the "Rumis," the light-skinned, Greek-speaking people of the Eastern Roman, or Byzantine, Empire (half conquered by the Turks in Rumi's day).

14 The sperm is pure, but the souls sent into bodies have hidden "defects," which cause their destinies to differ.

"I'm recognizing the people, one by one, just like wheat from barley in the mill,

"So that whoever is *to be* one of Paradise or whoever is *to be* an outsider is clear to me,[6] just as a snake and a fish are *clearly different.*"

During this *present* time *the verse*, "The Day[7] when faces will turn white and *others* will turn black" has become manifest to this band of people.[8]

Prior to this,[9] although the soul was full of defects, it was hidden in the womb *of the body* from the people *and* was invisible.

The miserable ones are those who were *decreed to be* miserable in their mother's womb.[10] Their condition is known from the marks on *their* bodies.[11]

The body *is* like a mother, pregnant with the infant of the soul. *And* death is the suffering and turmoil of being "born."

All the souls *who have* passed on[12] are waiting so that *they may see in* what manner that insolent soul will be born *into the next world.*

The *dark spirits of the* Ethiopians say, "It is ours." *And* the *light spirits of the* Anatolians[13] say, "It is very beautiful."

When it is born into the world of spirit and generosity, then disagreement *among* the white and black *spirits* no longer remains.

If it is an Ethiopian *spirit*, the Ethiopians drive it *toward them. And* the Anatolian also carries off *any spirit from* Anatolia from amid *the arriving souls.*

As long as it isn't "born" *into the Hereafter*, there are difficulties for *the people of* the world—*since* the one who can recognize *the destiny of* the "unborn" is scarce.

But he [*who is able*] sees by the light of God, since he has a way *to see* underneath the skin.

The essence of sperm juice is white and good.[14] But the reflection of the Anatolian or *of* the Ethiopian spirit

(*continued on page 97*)

15 "Certainly, We have created mankind in the best of upright forms. Then, we reduce him to the lowest of the low" (Q. 95:4–5).

16 The Day of Judgment will make clear the distinction between those who deserve to go to Paradise and those who deserve to go to Hell.

17 These trees symbolize the pious (date palms) who produce good fruits in the Hereafter and the wrongdoers (willows) who do not produce fruit.

18 "The People of the Left Hand": Those who are to be punished in Hell (Q. 56:41).

19 Severing of the hands is the Islamic punishment for repeated theft (although it is not applied in cases of starvation and mass famine). The hand that is punished in this manner is the one that stole: the right hand. Loss of the right hand is also shameful because greetings are made with the right hand only, since the left hand is used to clean (traditionally, using stones) after defecation.

Gives color to "the best of upright forms" *in the one case and* carries this *other* half *down* to "the lowest[15] *of the low.*"

This speech does not have *an* end. Ride back, so we aren't left *behind* by the train *of camels* in the caravan.

"*On* the Day when faces will turn white and *others* will turn black," it will make[16] the *difference between the pale* "Turk" and the *dark* "Hindu" generally known among the people [*gathered on the Day of Judgment*].

In the womb *of the body the difference between* "Hindu" and *"*Turk" is not clear. *But* when one is "born" *into the Hereafter, the observer there* can see him as *either* miserable or great.

Zayd continued: "I see clearly all of the men and women revealed [*as to their fate*], just as *it will be on* the Day of Resurrection.

"Look, shall I *keep* talking, or shall I shut *my* breath?" The Prophet bit his *own* lip, meaning, "Enough!"

Zayd continued, "O Messenger of God, shall I tell the secret of the Gathering *on the Day of Judgment?* Today, shall I make public to the world *the mystery of* the Revival *of the dead?*

"Leave me *unhindered,* so that I may tear up the *concealing* veils, *and* so that my pearl-like nature may shine like a sun.

"So that the sun may become eclipsed by me, *and* so that I may reveal *the difference between* the date palm and the willow tree.[17]

"I will reveal the mystery of the Resurrection, of the true coin, and of the true coin mixed with counterfeit,

"*And of* the People of the Left Hand[18] *with their* hands severed.[19] I will reveal openly the color of denying unbelief and the color of fraud and deceit.

(*continued on page 99*)

20 See n. 5 above on the Seven Hells.

21 This refers to mystical illumination.

22 The intermediate state is where souls wait after physical death until the Resurrection.

23 The Fountain of Kawthar is a blessed fountain in Paradise (mentioned in Q. 108:1), which satisfies all thirsts.

24 Those who are not allowed near the Fountain of Kawthar are thus denied the refreshing reward of being in Paradise.

25 These are the pure companions (sometimes called virgins) of Paradise (Q. 44:54; 52:20)—one of several Qur'anic metaphors for heavenly bliss).

26 This refers to the verse "And turn toward your Sustaining Lord and surrender (your will) to Him, before the punishment (of your rejection) comes to you. For then (after that) you will not be helped.... So that a soul will exclaim, 'Oh, misery for me, for what I disregarded (of my obligations) toward God!'" (Q. 39:54, 56).

27 The Prophet twisted the upper hem of his shirt or gown, in order to signal him to stop saying things that should not be spoken.

28 A verse in the Qur'an reads, "Certainly, that (behavior) of yours might offend the Prophet, and he might feel bashful of (asking) you (to leave). But God is not ashamed of (revealing) the truth [about the situation]" (Q. 33:53).

"I will open *the mystery* of the seven pits of hypocrisy[20] in the light of the Moon, which has no eclipse or waning.[21]

"I will openly reveal the coarse clothing of the wretched and contemptible, *and* will make audible the tambourines and kettledrums of the Prophets.

"I will bring clearly before the eyes of the rejecting disbelievers *the sight of* Hell, Paradise, and the intermediate *state*[22] in between *them*.

"I will reveal the surging Fountain of Kawthar,[23] which splashes *refreshingly* against their faces *while* its sound pulsates in *their* ears.

"And I will reveal clearly *in* this moment those persons who have been made to run, *remaining* thirsty, around it.[24]

"*I can feel* their shoulders rubbing against my shoulder, *and* their *desperate* shouts are coming into my ears.

"The people of Paradise are drawing one another into [*joyful*] embraces, out of free choice, *right* before my eyes.

"*And* they are visiting each other's seats of honor, *and* also robbing kisses from the lips[25] [*of the maidens of Paradise*].

"These ears of mine have become deaf from the *miserable* shouts of 'Oh, oh!' from the vile and corrupt ones *in Hell*, and by *their* screams of 'Oh, misery for me!'[26]

"These are *only* indications. I would speak *further* from the depths *of my experience*, but I'm afraid of the disapproval and censure of the Messenger *of God*."

Zayd was talking in this *ecstatic* manner, very "drunk" and disturbed. *Then* the Prophet gave *Zayd's* collar a twist.[27]

He said, "Be careful, *and* draw in *your reins!* For your horse has become *overheated. Your sense of* shame left *you* when the reflection of *the verse* 'God is not ashamed *of speaking the Truth*'[28] struck *upon your heart.*

"Your mirror has jumped out of *its* covering. The mirror and the scales can never speak contrary *to the truth.*"

(*continued on page 101*)

29 See chapter 8, n. 11.

30 Elsewhere, Rumi said, "If desire were to leap up within the mirror, the mirror would be like us in hypocrisy. (For) if the scale was desirous of wealth, the scale would never truthfully express the qualities of the condition (being measured)."

31 Laughing at another's beard or moustache is a Persian idiom, meaning to make fun of someone's vanity or foolishness.

32 Elsewhere, Rumi said, "See the (Holy) Mountain in (your) belly; (see) a chest (containing) the Sinai of Love."

33 Here is a play on "armpit" [*baghal*] and "deceit" [*daghal*].

34 "The King": God, who veils the sins of people so that they will have hope of His Mercy in the Hereafter.

35 Here Rumi begins his commentary.

36 "God is the one who made the ocean subject to you, so that ships may run in it by His command" (Q. 15:12). Humans have been given some (limited) power over nature in ways that yield benefits.

37 "And [in Paradise] they will be given to drink therein a cup [of wine] which is mixed with ginger [*Zanjabīl*], [and there is] a fountain therein named Salsabīl" (Q. 76:17–18).

The mirror and the scales can never close the breath *of their speech* for the sake of *avoiding* harm and shame to anyone.

The mirror and the scales *are* sublime and venerable touchstones,[29] so even if you perform services *to bribe them*[30] for two hundred years,

Saying, "Hide the truth, for my sake! Show increase and don't show decrease!"—

They will say to you, "Don't laugh at *your own* beard and moustache![31] *Can there be* a mirror and scales, and then fraud and *biased* advice?

"Since God has elevated us *in rank* for the *end result* that one is able to recognize the truth by *means of* us,

"If this was not *the case*, young man, what *would be* our worth? We would never be a decoration for the faces of the beautiful."

The Prophet continued, "But you should draw the mirror into *its* felt *covering* when He has made *your* chest a *Mount* Sinai by means of *spiritual* illumination."[32]

Zayd said, "But the Sunlight of Truth and the Sun of Eternity can never be contained under the armpit—

"*Since* it tears up both deceit as well as armpit,[33] *and* neither craziness nor reason can remain before it."

The Prophet replied, "If you place a single finger over an eye, it sees the world devoid of the sun.

"*Similarly*, a single tip of the finger becomes the moon's veil, and this is a sign of the veiling *power* of the King[34]—

"So that He can cause the world to be covered *by a little* spot, *and* the sun can become eclipsed by some *small piece of* rubbish *in the eye*."

Close your lips[35] and observe the depths of an ocean *within you, for* God made the ocean subject to the power of mankind[36]—

Just as the Fountain of Salsabīl and the *cups of Heavenly* ginger [37] are *going to be* under the control of the majestic inhabitants of Paradise.

(*continued on page* 103)

38 "A parable of the Garden which the righteous are promised: in it are rivers of incorruptible water; and rivers of milk, the taste of which never changes; and rivers of wine delightful to those who drink; and rivers of purified honey" (Q. 47:15).

39 Rumi says elsewhere, "Those rivers (in Paradise) also will flow at your command."

40 Someone limited to a particular object of love who loses it is left with nothing. But someone who discovers Universal Love has found something that transcends particular loves and is that person's Source.

41 Burāq was the miraculous steed upon which the Prophet rode during his Night Journey to Heaven (see *Mi'rāj* in the glossary).

The four rivers of Paradise[38] are *going to be* under our control. *Yet*, this *will* not *be* by our power, but by the Command of God.

We will keep them flowing *toward* anywhere we wish,[39] just like magic, according to the magician's desire.

And just as these two flowing fountains of *our* eyes are under the control of the heart and *under* the command of the soul.

If *the heart* wishes, *the person* goes toward poison and snakes. And if it wishes, *the person* goes toward trustworthy counsel.

If it wishes, *the person* goes toward objects perceived by the senses. And if it wishes, *the person* goes toward objects clothed [*in imagined forms*].

If it wishes, *the person* rides toward universals. And if it wishes, *the person* remains confined to particulars.[40]

The rest of the story about Zayd, regarding *his* answer to the Messenger *of God*—may God bless him and give him peace.

This speech lacks an end. *The Prophet said,* "Rise up, O Zayd, *and* tie a strap upon the Burāq[41] of your ability to speak.

"Since defects are disclosed *by means of your* talent for speech, it is tearing up the veils of hidden *matters.*

"*But* concealment has been required by God *for some time, so* drive *away* the drummer *and* block the road!

"Don't race *your mount, but* pull in the reins, *since* concealment is better. *It is* better *that* everyone *be* happy because of his own opinions.

"God requires that *even* His hopeless ones should not turn *their* faces from the worship *they continue to do.*

"*For* they become honored [*in their minds*] even with a *single* hope [*of reward in Heaven*], *so that* they run at its stirrup *for* a few days.

"*God* wills *for* that Mercy *of His* to shine on everyone, on the wrongdoers and the good, because of the universality of *His* Compassion.

(*continued on page 105*)

42 Islamic law is made up of the sacred laws revealed in the Qur'an and the example of the rulings, actions, and sayings of the Prophet.

43 This refers to the saying "My Companions are like the stars; whichever of them you follow, you will be (rightly) guided."

44 Meteors are depicted in the Qur'an (67:5) as driving away devils who try to overhear heavenly conversations between the angels regarding what is destined to happen on earth.

45 That is, at any time, such as (clairvoyantly) during the night or on dark and cloudy days.

46 "Ground, cloud, and shadow": Those who lack spiritual light.

47 "Say (O Muhammad), 'Truly, I am (only) a man like yourselves, but the Revelation has come to me that your God is One God'" (Q. 18:110; 41:6).

48 He means the revelation of the Qur'an, from God.

"*Therefore,* God wills that every prince and prisoner should be with hope, fear, and caution.

"This hope and fear are two veils, so that *people may be* nourished behind these veils.

"If you've torn the veils, fear and hope *will be* nowhere *to be found, and* the power and dominion of the Unseen *world will then have* become made public."

∽

Since the eyes of the faint-seeing person cannot bear *the direct light of* the sun, the stars have become *like* a candle for him so that he may find the way.

Concerning the speaking of the Prophet—may God pour blessings upon him and peace—to Zayd, saying, "Don't speak more openly *about* this mystery than this, and pay attention to following Islamic law."[42]

The Prophet said, "My Companions are *like* the stars[43] *in the sky:* candles for *the guidance of* travelers, and meteors *for stoning* satans."[44]

If anyone were to have the eyes and power *so that* he might obtain light *directly* from the sun[45] of the heavens,

There would have been no need for the star, O wretched one, to have been evidence for the light of the sun.

The Prophet who is like the Moon is saying to the ground, cloud, and shadow,[46] "I have been a man *like you, but* the Revelation has come to me.[47]

"I was dark in *my* nature, *just* like you, *but* the Revelation of the Sun[48] gave a light such as this to me.

"In regard to the suns [*of the invisible spiritual world*], I have a darkness, *yet* I have light for the sake of *illuminating* the darkness of souls.

(*continued on page 107*)

49 The advice is not to become hated by displaying his knowledge of the future to the public. A famous Sufi master counseled, "Don't ever seek fame, since fame is (the cause of) misfortune and calamity."

50 In mosques and Muslim homes, people remove their shoes in an entry hall. Here, it is a symbol for the base material world.

51 This is a word play on the words for "straw" and "galaxy." The meaning is that he has become "annihilated" of self, with no trace to be found.

52 "Our King": God.

"It is because of the [relative] weakness of my light that you can accept the brightness [that I bring], since you aren't the man for enduring the most luminous Sun."

∾

This speech lacks an end. Where is Zayd, so that I may give him advice, by saying, "Don't seek notoriety!"[49]

The return to the story of Zayd

You can't find Zayd now, since he has run away. He has leaped away from the row of shoes[50] and thrown off his sandals.

Who are you to find him? Zayd can't even find himself, like the star upon which the sun has shone.

You won't find a mark of him or a sign, just as you won't find a straw[51] in the Milky Way galaxy.

Our limited senses and speech are erased by the Light of the Knowledge of our King.[52]

Sayings of the Prophet

1 "My eyes are sleeping": This means that the heart of the Prophet was always in a state of remembrance, love, and worship of God.

2 This refers to both psychological and spiritual faculties of perception.

3 A saying of the Prophet reads, "I have a time with God in which I am not encompassed by any Prophet sent (by God), nor by any angel of (divine) nearness."

4 This is a reference to the saying of the Prophet regarding his continuous fasting: "My Lord gives me food and drink during the night."

5 The ritual prayer, done five times every day by Muslims, was revealed to the Prophet during his Night Journey (see *Mi'rāj* in the glossary).

6 This refers to the special nearness of the Prophet to God during his prayers.

7 During the Night Journey (see *Mi'rāj* in the glossary), the angel Gabriel was unable to accompany the Prophet closer to the Divine Presence.

13 □ Prayer and Guidance

Sometimes my state is similar to sleep; someone gone astray may think it is sleep.

Although my eyes are asleep, know *that* my heart is awake; *despite* my inactive appearance, know *that I am involved* in action.

Just as the Prophet said, "My eyes are sleeping, *but* my heart does not sleep *in forgetfulness* of the Lord of mankind."[1]

Your eyes are awake, and *yet your* heart is asleep in a dream. My eyes are asleep, *but* my heart *is* at the opening of the gate [*of Divine Grace*].

There are five other senses[2] for my heart, and this world and the next are the viewing place of the senses of *my* heart.

O you who have said, "I have a time"[3] every night "in the presence of your Lord." Give more explanation about that *spiritual* "soup,"[4] O my Prophet!

Finally, the Prophets have produced *rituals of* prayer. Now, this Prophet *of ours,* who has produced the *Islamic* ritual prayer,[5] said this: "I have a time with God[6] in which I am not encompassed by any Prophet sent *by God,* nor by any angel of *divine* nearness." Therefore, we know that the soul of ritual prayer is not only the form, but it is *a state of* being "drowned" and unaware *of the world,* so that all these *material* forms remain outside *of this state* and are not contained there. Even *the angel* Gabriel, who is pure spiritual reality, cannot be contained *there.*[7]

(continued on page 113)

8 According to Islamic Law, a ritual prayer is complete if a minimum number of required actions are done. However, pious Muslims (especially Sufis) seek to have total concentration on the Presence of God while praying.

9 A saying of the Prophet reads, "O God, show us the true as the true, and provide us with the means to follow it. And show us the false as the false, and provide us with the means to avoid it."

10 This refers to the Prophet's sincerity in wanting to know the truth.

11 "O God, show us things as they are" is quoted in Arabic, and then Rumi interprets the saying in Persian.

12 See chapter 4, n. 51.

13 This refers to the Prophet's saying, "Truly I seek the forgiveness of God seventy times in every day."

14 It is said that the Prophet repented of anything that distracted him from full awareness of the Presence of God—even the duties of teaching and guiding others.

∽

Listen to *one* of the traditions of *Muhammad* the Chief of Chiefs: "No ritual prayer is complete except with presence *of the mind on God.*"[8]

∽

Because of this, Muhammad requested *a favor* from God, saying, "Show *me* the ugly as the ugly and the true as the true,[9]

"So that at the end, when You turn the page, I will not fall into restlessness and agitation from remorse."

∽

Since its appearance has become changed, *and* since you are understanding it by these *imperfect* eyes,

O Lord! Show it as it is![10] Muhammad begged from God like this.

∽

If everything were to appear just as it was, the Prophet *who was* possessed of penetrating and illumined vision would not have called out, "O God, show us things as they *actually* are"[11]—*meaning*, "You show *something as* attractive, and in reality it is ugly, and You show *something as* ugly, and in reality it is surprisingly beautiful. Therefore, show us everything just as it is, so that we may not fall into the trap and *so that* we may not continually be going astray." Now, even though your opinion is good and luminously clear, it is not better than his judgment, *and* he spoke in this manner. Now, you shouldn't rely upon *just* any fancied idea or any opinion. Act humbly, and be *piously* fearing *of God.*[12]

∽

I am repenting seventy times a day,[13] like the Prophet, because of speaking and offering *teachings.*[14]

(continued on page 115)

15 The Prophet said, "Gain fulfillment through prayer from tender-hearted (feeling)." After quoting this in Arabic, Rumi paraphrases and explains it in Persian.

16 Children are tricked: Such as by eagerly exchanging a pearl for walnuts and raisins (*Math.*, VI:3466).

17 Rostam was a legendary hero and warrior in Persian literature.

18 See *mu'min* in the glossary.

19 This line refers to a Hadīth, "The (true) believer is discerning, shrewd, and cautious."

∞

The Messenger—may God pour blessings and peace upon him—said: "The moment that your hearts are afflicted, your eyes are full of tears, and burning *of longing desire* and *humble* neediness become evident—in that moment, *which* is the time of needful desiring, you will have fulfillment."[15] Since in that moment, the door of *Divine* Mercy is open, wish for *your* needs *like that.*

∞

Children are tricked with walnuts and with raisins.[16] Otherwise, how are we suitable for *desiring* walnuts and sesame seeds?

If an old woman has hidden *herself* under a helmet and under armor *and* says, "I am *like* the most celebrated *hero* Rostam[17] of the battle lines"—

Everyone knows that she is a woman by her *movements of* attack and retreat. How can we make an error, when we are [*viewing*] in the Light of Muhammad?

Muhammad said such as this: "The *true* believer[18] is discerning."[19] Now close *your* mouth, since we are rightly guided advisers without *need of* speech.

∞

(*continued on page 117*)

20 The true believer is blessed with the insight into the difference between good and bad, right and wrong, and so on.

21 It is understood that Muslim Sufi saints and mystics receive divine insights and guidance, but it is not called "revelation" [*wahy*], a term reserved only for the Prophets. Instead, it is called "inspiration" [*ilhām*] and must not be contrary to the Islamic Revelation to be considered genuine.

22 This refers to the saying "The parable of my (religious) community is the likeness of the ship of Noah: the one who grabs (on to) it is rescued, and the one who remains behind is drowned."

23 "Spiritual Master" [*shaykh*]: A Sufi master and guide.

24 Rumi refers to a Muhammad-like Muslim Sufi master, a true successor to and follower of the Prophet in every generation. This refers to the Prophet's saying, "The elder [*shaykh*] among his followers is like the Prophet among his (religious) community."

25 When you are with a Spiritual Master: See n. 23 above.

26 Rumi means the Muslim saint who is the Prophet's successor in regard to spiritual perception and wisdom, and who can help save others from being drowned in the "Flood" of worldly desires.

Concerning that which has been said, *that* after Muhammad—may God pour blessings and peace upon him—and the Prophets—peace be upon them—Revelation does not descend *from God* upon others [*in the future*], why doesn't it? *Because* it is not plainly called "Revelation" *anymore*. In other words, it is *continuing*, but it is not *mentioned* by that quality. This is what the Prophet spoke *about when he said*, "The *true* believer sees by the Light of God."[20] When the believer is looking with the Light of God, he views everything just as it is. He sees the first, the last, the hidden, and the present—because he is gazing with the Light of God. He sees with the Light of God and by means of the Light of God nothing is hidden. For if it is hidden, that is not the Light of God. Therefore, the spiritual reality of Revelation exists, although it is not plainly called "Revelation." *Rather*, it is called "hidden revelation."[21]

In regard to this, the Prophet said, "I am like the ship in the flood of Time.

"I and my companions *are* like the ark of Noah: whoever thrusts *his* hand into *ours* [*for help*] will find *spiritual* openings and success."[22]

When you are with a spiritual Master,[23] you are far distant from rude and ugly *behavior*, you are a traveler and in a "ship," day and night.

Then you are under the *protecting* shelter of a life-giving spirit, you are *peacefully* asleep on the ship, *and* you are traveling on the Way.

Don't separate from the [*one who is like a*] prophet of your own days.[24] Don't lean *and depend* on your own skill and wishes.

That king of the Prophets said such as this: "I am the ship[25] in this universal Ocean,

"Or *else* someone who, in regard to *inward* perceptions, has become a true successor[26] in my place."

(*continued on page 119*)

27 This refers to a saying of the Prophet, "*Regarding* the one who makes his cares a *single* care, God will make the rest of his cares sufficient." Elsewhere, Rumi interpreted this in Persian: "He said, 'Go (away)! Whoever chooses *only* care for religion, God will sever (all) the rest of (his) cares from him.'"

28 The "row of lovers" refers to the true lovers of God. It also refers to a saying attributed by the Sufis to the Prophet (however, the word "Sufi" did not come into use until a couple of centuries later): "The one who wants to sit together with God should sit together with the people of Sufism."

29 In other words, "The world has become warm with religious fervor because of your devotion."

30 The one who fervently loves God is advised not to associate with those who deny or forget God, who are compared to ashes.

31 In another variation, the Prophet's saying ends, "(For) it may be that a breath from (among) them may reach you and you will not be unhappy after that forever." Here, Rumi especially means the beneficent influence of the Sufi saints.

32 He means that Divine Mercy is increasing with the Islamic era.

33 This relates to the Sufi teaching of the "spiritual moment": being aware of the present time, when spiritual grace, blessing, and realization may occur.

34 "The soul of fire": The soul full of worldly passions and cravings.

∞

I have been reciting from the speech of the Prophet only: "The one who makes his cares a *single* care."[27]

∞

God commanded in a revelation, "O Prophet,
"Don't sit on the way except in the row of lovers[28]
"Although the world has become warm because of your fire,[29]
"[*Even*] fire may die from association with ashes."[30]

∞

In explanation of the Tradition, "Truly, during the days of your time, your Lord has certain breaths[31] [*of Mercy*]. So meet them [*when they occur*]!"

The Prophet said, "God's Breaths *of Mercy* are increasing[32] during these days.

"*So* keep your ears and minds *alert* for these times,[33] *and* seize *the opportunity of* such breaths as these."

The breath *of Mercy* came, saw you, and left; it gave *spiritual* life to whomever it wished, and left.

Another breath has come. Be aware, so that you don't stay back from this *one* as well, O master of the house.

The soul of fire[34] found *itself* being extinguished by it, *and* from its permanence, the soul of the dead wore a robe [*of everlasting life*].

(*continued on page 121*)

35 Since Islam is the last Revelation, eventually the Muslims themselves will corrupt it (and no other religion will cause its decline), and then the Day of Judgment will come.

36 Rumi expresses the belief that he is living in the age of the Prophet Muhammad, the final Prophet sent by God to humanity before the Day of Judgment.

37 Rumi quotes Arabic words from the saying of the Prophet "I am the final (Prophet in time), (but) the foremost (in excellence) on the Day of Resurrection."

∞

The Prophet said this: "The stagnation of my *religious* community will be at the time of the corruption of my community."[35] In other words, "There is no Prophet after me whose *religious* community will be superior over my community, since my community obtained superiority over the communities of Jesus and Moses. And there is no religion that will make my religion obsolete and stagnant, since my religion will make previous religions obsolete."

∞

Therefore, see the divine kindnesses, since we have come (to the world) *during the final period of* time, at the end.[36]

For the final era is prior *in importance* to *the previous eras*—*as is mentioned* in the Prophet's saying, "The final *in time*, the foremost *in excellence*."[37]

1 The saying refers to a type of lute, perhaps played with a bow, or it may refer to a hollow wind instrument. The complete saying is that the true believer's voice lacks a good sound (to God) unless his stomach is empty, just as when the body of the viol is hollowed out.

2 The Prophet used to stand in prayer throughout much of the night until his feet became swollen. Rumi depicts the people near the mosque of Qubā as becoming ecstatic from the effects of the Prophet's spiritual devotions.

3 Literally, "slave" (of God), 'Abdu 'llāh (in Arabic), referring to one of the Prophet's most exalted titles (see, for example, Q. 17:1; 53:10).

4 This saying expresses Divine Omnipotence and determination of Destiny, yet other sayings (as well as verses from the Qur'an) encourage free will and the use of willpower. Therefore, Rumi rejects fatalism.

5 In other words, "Don't be passive because of extremist beliefs in Destiny and Fate, but use the amount of free will that you have been given in order to serve God."

14 □ Self-Denial and Ego-Death

When he became empty *of complaints*, he began to mention *the name of God*. He made the tune of "O Lord!" and "O Lord take me into Your protection!"

Because the Prophet said, "The *true* believer is *like* the lute,[1] which is a maker of sound at the time of being *made* empty."

Regarding Muhammad, *at* night he didn't eat, *yet* at dawn his stomach would be full. He would say, "I have become the guest of contentment."

The Prophet's feet were made swollen from standing *during most* of the night, until the people of Qubā tore *their* shirts because of his wakefulness.[2]

The saying of the *Prophet Muhammad, God's* servant,[3] "Whatever God wills occurs"[4] is not *intended* for *the interpretation* "Act like a lazy person about it."[5]

But rather it is *meant as* urging to sincere devotion and effort, meaning, "Be prepared for *doing* greater service [*to God*]."

(continued on page 125)

6 This is a reference to a saying of the Prophet: "My satan has submitted [*aslama*] to my power." It means that his self-willed egotism became a submitter (the literal meaning of the word *muslim*).

7 "Denying unbeliever": See *kāfir* in the glossary.

8 The shin would be a fairly worthless gift (a sheep's bone with little meat). Here, Rumi provides an example of the Prophet's exquisite manners and gentle compassion in his dealings with others.

9 This line refers to the Night Journey (see *Mi'rāj* in the glossary). "(Muhammad) did not swerve or turn away, for he certainly saw the greatest among the signs of his Lord" (Q. 53:17). This means that the Prophet never ceased being aware of the Presence of God during all his actions.

Listen to Muhammad, who said, "My devil became a Muslim;[6] it isn't *acting like* another denying unbeliever."[7]

Concerning *the saying of Muhammad* "My satan has *completely* submitted and become a Muslim," your base ego will have become lordly *and noble*—may such as this *come to* be!

It is in a narration *that* a horse was brought from a place near the sea to Muhammad—may God pour blessings and peace upon him. *It was* mentioned as a gift, *and its* price and stature *were* so great that *it was* worth the taxes of *an entire* province. He accepted *it and* said, "If I were offered a shin[8] *of a sheep's leg*, I would have accepted it." Muhammad—may God give him blessings and peace—is saying, "With this *attitude* of mine *of* freedom from *worldly* attachments, it is clear that the treasuries and riches of the world next to the treasuries and riches of the heavens— what *little* value it *all* is! Since this world picks at pieces of bread from the heavens. *And* those treasuries of the heavens and riches were offered to me, *but* I didn't glance *at them even* with the corner of my eye. *'His* sight did not swerve nor turn away.'"[9] *How* amazing *that for* someone who is experiencing *direct* encounter with God, anything *else* can be something *of value* in His Presence! "*Thus* I did *accept* this because of freedom from *worldly* attachments. However, because of generosity, graciousness, and a pleasing meeting with people, I would accept with honor anything brought to *my* presence as a gift, *even* a rabbit's leg. And I would not make the bringer *of the gift feel* dejected and disappointed." The Messenger of God spoke truthfully. *And* he accepted that gift of a horse.

(continued on page 127)

10 Here, Rumi interprets in Arabic the saying attributed to the Prophet as simply, "Die before death." This saying, quoted mainly by Sufis, is interpreted variously, such as "die" and don't give "life" to sinful desires so that you will not die and be in a state of suffering in the Hereafter; "die" to personal existence and egotism in this life so that you may taste of the joys of Paradise before death.

11 This paraphrases a saying that refers to one who has experienced mystical "death" before physically dying. See also n. 10 above on the saying "Die before death."

12 He has contentment with whatever God provides, as well as having "poverty" or nothingness of ego in the Presence of God. "O man, you are poor in relation to God, and God is the Rich, the Praiseworthy" (Q. 35:15).

13 In this saying, the Prophet meant (among other meanings) that God honored him because of his humble submission to whatever God provided. He often had very little to feed his family, he lived very simply, and he was empty of selfish motives.

14 The wax candle completely dissolves into the flame and becomes entirely "light," so that it can no longer have a shadow. This is Rumi's response to preceding verses in which it is asked how one can escape from himself if his own shadow is his enemy. Rumi answers with a metaphor for mystical annihilation of the self of the lover of God in the divine light.

Death before death is safety, O young man, *and* Muhammad has told us such.

He said, "All of you should die before death[10] comes *and* you die with afflictions."

∞

In regard to this, Muhammad said, "O seeker of *divine* secrets! Do you wish to see a dead one who is living?[11]

"He continues to travel upon the rubbish heap of the world—dead, *yet* his soul has *already* gone *up* to the Heavens.

"*At* this *very* moment there is a dwelling for his soul up above, *so that* if he dies, his spirit isn't transported.

"Because it has made a transition prior to death—*but* this may be understood *only* by 'dying,' not by *using* the mind.

"It is a transition, *but* not like the transition of the souls of the common people. *Rather,* it is like a transition from one *spiritual* dwelling to another place."

∞

When annihilation adorns him, because of *his spiritual* poverty,[12] he becomes Muhammad like, without a shadow.

Since annihilation is the adornment for *the one attaining the state of* "Poverty is my pride,"[13] he becomes without a shadow like the candle flame.

When the candle becomes entirely flame, from head to foot, there is no *way of* passage around it for the shadow.[14]

Then the wax escapes into the light from *both* itself and the shadow, for the sake of him who poured *the wax into the mold.*

(*continued on page 129*)

15 Rumi paraphrases in Persian this saying attributed by Sufis to the Prophet: "The one who has known himself truly has known his Sustaining Lord." It is interpreted variously in such ways as these: whoever has known himself as a powerless and needy servant has known God as the Source of all help and bounty; whoever has known his own attributes has known God as the Source of all attributes; whoever has known his self [*nafs*] as non-existent has known God as the only Existence and Reality.

∞

In relation to that, the Prophet has made this explanation: "Whoever has known himself has known God."[15]

1 This is a paraphrase in Persian of a saying of the Prophet, who related that God said, "My earth does not contain Me, nor do My Heavens, but the heart of My believing servant contains Me." And in another version: "My earth does not contain Me, and My Heavens do not (either), but the heart of My believing, pious, pure, and self-restrained servant does contain Me." These "Divine Sayings" are not in the Qur'an.

2 Verses in the Qur'an describe the divine message of joy welcoming the righteous souls into Paradise: "O soul (in a state of) tranquillity! Return to your Lord, well satisfied and pleasing (to God)! Enter among My servants and enter My Paradise!" (Q. 89:27–30).

3 This refers to a divine saying: "(God) said, 'I was a Hidden Treasure, and then I loved that I might be known, and then I created the creation so that I might be known.'"

4 The Prophet reported that God told him during the Night Journey (see *Mi'rāj* in the glossary), "If not for you, I would not have created the Heavens." This refers to the creation of the universe. It is also interpreted by the Sufis as addressed to the saint who fully reflects God's Attributes.

15 □ Divine Sayings

The Prophet related that "God has said: 'I am not ever contained within "high" or "low."

"'I am also not contained within the earth or the Heavens. Know this for sure, O precious one.

"'Yet I am contained in the heart of the *true* believer.[1] How wondrous! If you are seeking Me, *then* search within those hearts.'"

God *also* said, "'Enter among My servants,'[2] *where* you will encounter a Paradise including a vision of Me, O reverently pious one!"

Muhammad was saying to God, "Since You are without need of us, what was the wisdom in creating all these things—tell *the reason* at last!"

God said, "O Life of the World, I was a treasure very much hidden,[3] *and* I wanted that treasure of Goodness and Generosity to become revealed."

Pure Love was joined to Muhammad *because* God told him, "If not for you"[4]—for the sake of Love.

(continued on page 133)

5 In the story of the Prophet's Night Journey into Heaven (see *Mi'rāj* in the glossary), he is said to have reached the "utmost limit" (Q. 53:14), where it said that even the angel Gabriel could not accompany him any farther. The Night Journey is also called the Heavenly Ascension.

6 Rumi interprets the divine saying "If not for you" (see n. 4 above).

7 This expresses the profound mystical teaching in Sufism that God's Attributes may be reflected in the holy prophets and saints, for whom God is the intimate Friend and Beloved.

8 Rumi makes a pun on a different meaning of the word "witness," which refers to an attractive person who is the object of fond gazes. Here, the pure heart of the saint is called the place of witnessing God's Self-Revelation.

9 Erotic imagery is used to symbolize the intimacy of God with His "concubine slaves"—His prophets, saints, and mystics who are the "witnesses" of His own attributes of Beauty.

10 This means the love-play of hiding Himself in the "folds of creation" from His would-be lovers, or spiritual seekers.

Because he was unique *in reaching* the "utmost limit" in Love.⁵ Thus, *God* made him special among the prophets,

Saying, "If it was not for the sake of pure Love,⁶ I would not have given any existence to the Heavens.

"For that *purpose,* I elevated the high Heavens so that you may understand the exaltedness of Love."

"The Most Just" is the Name of God, and *so the saint who is called* "witness" belongs to Him, *since* he is the just witness. *And* from this point of view, he is the eye of the Friend.⁷

The heart *of the saint* is the place of God's *Self* revelation in this world and the next, since the king's gaze reaches the beloved *favorite.*⁸

God's Love and the secret of His *amorous* play with "beautiful beloveds"⁹ were the source of all His [*hiding Himself through*] making "veils."¹⁰

Thus, for that reason our *Lord,* who is amorously playful with *His* beloveds, said, "If not for you" during the *Prophet's* encounter on the night of the Ascension.

The Heavens are revolving around Love. Leap up, so we may also whirl!

Can you see whom God spoke *about* when *He said,* "If not for you, I would not have created *the universe*"? Muhammad the Chosen is the Mine of Love.

Let's wheel around Love for a while. How much *longer* shall we revolve around this dead carcass *of the body?*

Praises of the Prophet

1 Rumi testifies his belief in the basic creed of Islam. The first half is often chanted by Sufis (silently or vocally, individually or in a group, sitting in a circle or standing shoulder to shoulder). For the Sufis, this phrase has a number of meanings, such as these: there is no power but His Power, no love but His Love, no beauty but His Beauty, no reality but His Reality, no true existence but His Existence.

2 "Truly God and His angels send blessings upon the Prophet. (So) O you who believe, pray for blessings upon him and greet (him) with (wishes for) peace" (Q. 33:56). In this verse, Muslims are told to pray for blessings upon the soul of the Prophet Muhammad, out of gratitude for the debt they owe to him for his service to God.

3 This line occurs in a story about a debtor who took his wealthy benefactor for granted but became unable to pay his debts when the man died. Here the benefactor is used as a symbol of the generosity of the Prophet.

4 The Prophets and Messengers include all the Prophets of God, known and unknown. The Qur'an states that a Messenger has been sent to every people (Q. 10:47) and that Muhammad is the "Seal of the Prophets," the final Prophet before the Day of Judgment (Q. 33:40).

5 The prayer for blessings upon the descendants and family of Muhammad is also understood to include his true spiritual descendants.

16 □ Affirmations and Blessings

And I bear witness that "there is no divinity except God" (Q. 47:19; 36:35), the sole *divinity* who has no partners. And I bear witness that "Muhammad is the Messenger of God"[1] (Q. 33:40; 48:29).

For this reason, God said, "Pray for [*Me to send*] blessings upon him,"[2] since Muhammad was the [*generous*] one to whom *debts were* transferred.[3]

And may God pour blessings upon Muhammad and upon all of the Prophets and Messengers![4] Amen, O Lord of *all* the worlds!

And *all* praise is to God alone! And may God pour blessings upon our chief, Muhammad, and his descendants and his family![5] "And God is sufficient for us and the most excellent Guardian" (Q. 3:173).

(*continued on page 139*)

6 | This is understood to include his true followers in every generation.

7 | The famous Night Journey in which the Prophet was taken up to Heaven by the angel Gabriel (see *Mi'rāj* in the glossary).

8 | It has been said of Rumi that "When he was becoming (spiritually) drunk in the mystical concert [*samā'*], he would grab hold of the singers [to stop singing], and while whirling and stamping his foot (rhythmically), he would offer the blessings: 'O God, pour blessings upon Muhammad and upon the family of Muhammad!' Then he would begin [the mystical concert] again."

9 | The "branch of candy" is an idiom that refers to the custom, during one of the two Islamic religious festivals of the year (at the end of the fasting month of Ramadān and after the Pilgrimage [Hajj] rites in Mecca), of offering a gift of rock candy stuck to a little branch.

10 | The Fountain of Eternal Youth was a fabled spring of water said to confer immortality to the one who drinks from it. Rumi uses it as a symbol of the source of spiritual renewal for the soul.

11 | Giving alms to the poor is one of the Five Pillars of Islam, which include the creed (worshiping no god but the One God and acknowledging Muhammad as the Prophet of God), the five daily prayers, the annual monthlong fast of Ramadān, and the Pilgrimage [Hajj] to Mecca once in one's lifetime, if it can be afforded.

12 | It is an Islamic custom to bless and praise the Prophet Muhammad by means of poetry and song during the two Islamic festivals.

And may God bless the most excellent of His creatures, Muhammad, his descendants, companions,[6] and family and bestow peace *upon all of them!*

Just as, during the night of the Ascension,[7] God made *the greeting of peace* with the Light of the Absolute upon Muhammad: "Peace be upon you."

I bring blessings upon you,[8] *O Muhammad, so* that the breeze of nearness *to God* may increase. Since, with nearness of the Whole, all parts are allowed to approach.

Suddenly, there grew a "branch of candy."[9]
And suddenly, there bubbled such a Water of *Everlasting* Life.[10]
Suddenly, there flowed alms *to the poor*[11] from the king.
May there be joy for the soul of Muhammad, and greetings *of peace!*[12]

(continued on page 141)

13 That is, the attributes of the material world; in particular, the attributes of the human body and personality.

14 See *Nūr-i Muhammad* in the glossary.

15 Rumi usually calls the Prophet by this title, "Mustafā," which means "the Chosen" (Prophet of God).

The spirit which was bound within the form of attributes[13]

Went to the *Divine* Essence by means of the Light of *Muhammad*[14] the Chosen.[15]

The moment it started going, it said out of joy,

"Blessings *be* on the joyful spirit of *Muhammad* the Chosen!"

1 "Beloved of God" is a title of the Prophet Muhammad. According to the Mevlevi ("whirling dervish") tradition in Turkey, this ode was composed by Rumi (however, it is not in the early manuscripts of Rumi's *Dīvān*). It is called "The Noble Praise (of the Prophet)" and is sung at the beginning of every Whirling Prayer Ceremony. It incorporates praises of Rumi preceding, intermixed with, and following these six verses in praise of the Prophet.

2 Rumi refers to the Prophet's Night Journey (see *Mi'rāj* in the glossary).

3 "Religious Law" is the Islamic law, based on the Qur'an and the model of the Prophet's example (see *Sharī'at* in the glossary).

4 Rumi's spiritual master, Shams-i Tabrīzī, commemorated the Prophet Muhammad in his heart, presumably by the traditional practice of repeating prayers to God to send blessings and peace upon the Prophet.

5 This title ("Chosen") was used to refer only to the Prophet (see *Muhammad* in the glossary).

17 □ Praises and Virtues

O Beloved of God,[1] you are the Messenger of the Sole Creator! You are the one chosen by the Holy Lord of Majesty *Who is* without equal.

You are the delight of the Lord God *and* the highest Full Moon of created beings, *and* you are the light of the eyes of *God's* Messengers *and* the Lamp of our eyes.

On the night of the Ascension,[2] *the angel* Gabriel was at *your* stirrup, *and* you are *the one who was* standing on top of the nine blue domes *of Heaven.*

O Messenger of God, you know *that* your community are deprived and destitute, *and* you are the guide of those who are vulnerable and helpless.

You are the cypress tree of the rose garden of Prophethood *and* the spring season of spiritual knowledge.

You are the rosebush of the garden of the Religious Law[3] and the nightingale of the lofty *Heavens!*

Shams-i Tabrīzī *is one* who has the praise of the Messenger[4] in *his* heart. O Chosen *Prophet of God,*[5] you are the supreme master!

(continued on page 145)

6   This also refers to the Prophet's Night Journey to the Divine Throne (see *Mi'rāj* in the glossary).

7   "Mercy to (all) peoples": Words addressed by God to Muhammad (Q. 21:107).

8   These words are spoken in a story about the Prophet's grandfather, who described the infant Muhammad in a prayer.

The Chosen Prophet, sublime mediator *with God,* the one admitted *to the Divine Presence as in the verse* "he approached and came nearer" (Q. 53:8), the elect of the elect of *the one who approached up to* "the space of two bow lengths or nearer"[6] (Q. 53:9), Muhammad the Chosen, the best of those who are foremost and last, the Seal of the Prophets, the most select of created beings, the place of manifestation of "Clear Signs *of God*" (Q. 22:16), the Ocean without limit or measure, the Sun of *the verse* "We made him a Light so that he may walk among the people" (Q. 6:122), the key to Paradise and Gardens; the revealer of the secrets and mysteries of *divine* realities, the illuminator of the illuminated ones *and* the royal seal of the possessor of "Truly We gave you O *Muhammad* the *Heavenly* Fountain *of Grace*" (Q. 108:1)—may the blessings of God be upon him and upon his good pure family...

There has never been a beauty like that of a *Prophet like* Muhammad in this world or the next. May the Glory of God help him!

A voice from the lofty ones *among the angels came* from Heaven to every beggar: "O pure spirit of the one who is followed! O Mercy to *all* peoples!"[7]

Yet, I have seen[8] the signs of Your Grace and Kindness in the appearance of that incomparable Pearl, O Generous One.

Since, although he is from *among* us, he doesn't resemble us. We are entirely *like* copper, and Muhammad is *like* the *alchemical* elixir.

(continued on page 147)

9 The Holy Veranda refers to the roof of the "Marvelously Built Temple," the heavenly counterpart of the temple in Mecca called the Ka'ba.

10 "Fire and smoke" are the anger and cravings and the density and darkness of ordinary human nature.

11 "And the East and West (and all directions) belong to God. For whichever way you turn, there is the Face of God. Truly God is All-Encompassing, All-Knowing" (Q. 2:115).

12 This phrase refers to a heart opened by God to understand divine knowledge and love. Such "chest opening" is an image in the Qur'an (see 94:1; 20:25). When the "eye of the heart" is opened, that person will see everything by the Light of God.

When Muhammad opened the door of the wine room of the Unperceived *world,* a great decline of sales for pure wine occurred *in the marketplace.*

Learn an alchemy from the Prophet: be accepting with whatever God gives you.

For He will open the door of Paradise *in* the same moment when you become satisfied during *trials of* affliction and difficulty.

Whoever has a soul purified from *worldly* cravings will quickly see the Presence *of God* and the Holy Veranda.[9]

When Muhammad became purified of this fire and smoke[10] *of worldly desires,* every place he faced was the Face of God.

But since you are the companion of the temptations of *Satan* the evil-wishing one, how can you know *the meaning of the verse* "There is the Face of God"?[11]

Everyone who has the "door" of *his* chest truly open[12] will see a hundred suns in the sky of the heart.

The Prophet was exceedingly humble, because all the fruits of this world and the next were gathered together for him, *so* he was undoubtedly more humble than all. He said, "No one preceded the Messenger in the greeting of peace." *This means,* a person is never able to offer the greeting of peace upon the Prophet before the Prophet *offers,* because the Prophet was quick in doing *it* out of extreme humility and would give the greeting *first.* And even if, supposing, he didn't give the greeting first, still he would be humble. And *even in this case* he would be preceding in *offering* the greeting, because they learned and heard the greeting of

(continued on page 149)

13 When the Prophet's army conquered Mecca (with hardly a fight), he ordered the 360 idols within the Ka'ba to be destroyed. Likewise, he strove to eradicate any beliefs that the One God has any partners or associates (including subdeities viewed as "sons" or "daughters" of God).

14 The inward idol refers to forms of self-worship of one's ego, such as pride, reputation, justification of anger, jealousy, and selfish desires.

15 "That power": The power of your pure monotheistic faith gained as a result of the Prophet's mission.

16 Wine (forbidden in Islam) is a metaphor in Sufi poetry for the bliss of Paradise, symbolized in the Qur'an as "rivers of wine delightful to those who drink it" (47:15).

peace from him. All *that* the peoples of former and later times possess *is* from his reflection. And they are *part of* his shade.

Muhammad broke many idols in the world,[13] so that *religious* communities were saying, "O *our Sustaining* Lord!"

If it had not been for Muhammad's efforts, you also would have worshiped idols like your ancestors.

This head of yours has escaped from prostrating to idols, so that you may recognize his claim *of gratitude* upon the *religious* community.

If you speak, talk about gratitude for this liberation, *so* that he may also free you from the inward idol.[14]

Because he freed your head from *worship of* idols, you should also liberate *your* heart by means of that power.[15]

The Companions *of the Prophet* who went *into battle half* naked before the swords [*of the polytheists*] were "drunk and demolished" by [*the "wine" of*] Muhammad the Chosen.

I spoke in error—*rather* Muhammad was not the cupbearer; he was a cup full of "wine,"[16] and God was the Cupbearer of the virtuous ones.

1 In Islam, all love comes from God: "For truly my Lord is All-Compassionate, All-Loving" (Q. 11:90); "For You are the Most Merciful of the merciful" (Q. 7:151). The life of the Prophet Muhammad is filled with instances of love and compassion. In Islamic mysticism, loving God as Divine Love and the Most-Loving is especially emphasized. In this respect, Muslim mystics have viewed themselves as lovers, God as the Beloved, and God's Love as the origin of the universe and all things.

2 "Our rejecting natures": Literally, "unbelieving natures." See *kāfir* (unbeliever) in the glossary.

3 "The seven heavens and the earth and (all) that is therein glorify Him, and there is not a thing but celebrates His praise, but you do not understand their praise" (Q. 2:115).

4 Bilāl was the Ethiopian companion of the Prophet, whom the latter selected to be the first to recite the call to prayer to invite the Muslims to prepare for each of the five daily prayers.

18 □ Love and Closeness with God

Love is the path and road of our Prophet.[1]
We were born from love and love was our mother.
O you *who are* our mother, *you are* hidden within veils,
Concealed from our rejecting natures.[2]

Similarly, to the Prophet, this world is drowned in the praise and glorification *of God*,[3] but to us, *it is* unaware and ignorant *of God*.

To his eyes, this world is full of love and favors, *but* to the eyes of others it is dead and inanimate.

The Chief of the Pilgrimage of Love has arrived, the Messenger of the Ka'ba of good fortune. He freed you from [*the effects of*] every evil man and woman [*you may meet*] on the Way.

Grab the cloak of Muhammad the Messenger, *and* hear the call to prayer of Love every moment from the soul of Bilāl.[4]

We learned the skill of being a *true* man from God. We are the heroes of Love and the companions of Muhammad.

(continued on page 153)

5 All those, such as polytheists, who reject the One and Only God (see *kāfir* in the glossary).

6 This affirms Rumi's belief that the actions and words of the Prophet were inspired by God, as the Qur'an says: "And (Muhammad) does not speak (revelation) according to his desire; truly it is (nothing) except an inspired revelation" (Q. 53:3).

∞

This Love *is* like the spirit in this alien rubbish heap *of the world;* it resembles Muhammad *when he has* arrived among the rejecting unbelievers.[5]

∞

The Prophet—may God pour blessings and peace upon him and his family—when he used to become "drunk" and devoid of selfhood from ecstatic attractions to God *and* then would speak, he would say, "God Most High said." Consider well now: his tongue was speaking by way of *physical* form, but there was no "he-ness" in the midst. *For* in reality, the speaker was God Most High. When he was seeing himself at the beginning [*of receiving Revelation*], he was ignorant and lacking information about such words. *But now that* such words were being born from him— meaning that among his most select companions, they knew, "He isn't what he was at first, *for* this was *done under* the control of God"— Muhammad was giving such information about people and Prophets of the past *who lived* so many thousands of years before the existence of his own external form, and *even* up to the final era of the world which will come to be. And *he was telling* about the *Divine* Throne and Footstool and about the emptiness and fullness [*of unseen places*], *and* his being was seeing those things. *Someone* can never speak about these things *when* his being is newly created yesterday. *And* the recent can never give information about the eternal. Therefore, it became known that he was not speaking, *but* God was speaking. "And he does not speak out of *his own* desire. Truly it is *not* but a revealed revelation" (Q. 53:3–4).

∞

Because of that, whatever is said by the speech of Muhammad, the words are spoken *in reality* by the Ocean.[6]

(*continued on page 155*)

7 Muhammad spent much solitary time praying in a cave before he received the first Revelation and the divine command to be a Messenger to the people.

All of his spoken words were pearls of *that* Ocean, since there was an opening to the Ocean for his heart.

And He made Muhammad *to be* occupied with Himself at first.[7] After that, He commanded, "Call the people [*to the One God*], offer advice, and reform *them.*" Muhammad—may the blessings of God be upon him—was groaning and lamenting, "Ah, O Lord! What sin have I done? Why are You driving me from Your Presence? I have no wish for *involvement with* the people." God Most High said, "O Muhammad, do not grieve, for I will not leave you *so* that you become involved *only* with the people, *for* in the very essence of that involvement you will be with Me. And *even* a single hair from that [*total*] which you are *having* this time with Me will not be decreased when you come to *be involved with* the people. In every activity *in* which you are engaged, you will be in essential connection *with Me.*"

So that your soul may continue to laugh *with joy* endlessly, like the pure soul of Muhammad with the One *God*.

1 The Qur'an contains a verse (36:65) about the inability of the unbelievers (see *kāfir* in the glossary) to defend their errors on the Day of Judgment. But Rumi focuses on the meaning in this life: how hearts remain closed ("sealed") from speaking and receiving divine truth.

2 The Prophet is called the "Seal of the Prophets" by God (Q. 33:40): the last of the series of Prophets (such as Noah, Abraham, Moses, and Jesus) before the Day of Judgment.

3 The restraints would be raised so that the mouths of their souls might be opened to receive the nourishment of spiritual knowledge.

4 Rumi affirms that Muhammad is the final Prophet and that previous religions founded by Prophets are superseded by Islam.

5 This verse (Q. 48:1) refers to a treaty made with the pagans of Mecca, which was a great victory. Rumi interprets God's Revelation to Muhammad as including spiritual openings and victories.

6 Rumi refers to the belief in the Prophet's intercession with God (with His permission), as in the verse "The Prophet…is a mercy to those among you who believe" (Q. 9:61).

7 The people in Paradise may contemplate directly the "full moon" of divine beauty.

19 □ The Seal of the Prophets

This is the meaning of *the verse* "We will set a seal on their mouths."[1] *And* this understanding is important for the wayfarer *on the spiritual path,*

So that by his *following* the path of the Seal of the Prophets,[2] the heavy restraints might perhaps be raised from his lips.[3]

Any seals which the Prophets *of the past* left *in place* have been taken off[4] by the religion of Muhammad.

The unopened locks had also remained *in place and* were opened by the power of *the verse* "Truly, We have opened *for you.*"[5]

Muhammad is the Intercessor for this world and the next world[6]—*in* this world for religion, and there for the Gardens *of Paradise.*

In this world, he says *the prayer* "May You show them the way!" And in that world he says, "May You show them the moon!"[7]

(*continued on page 159*)

8 This was a frequent prayer of the Prophet.

9 Muhammad is the foremost of the Prophets (as well as the last Prophet) sent by God. See n. 2 above.

10 "Openings" means spiritual success, victory, revelation, happiness, and the opening of the human heart to the light of divine wisdom.

11 The Prophet was the vice-regent of God, and his successors were rulers of the Islamic state. Rumi refers to the Muslim saints (Sufis) who are the Prophet's spiritual descendants.

12 Baghdād is in 'Irāq; Herāt is in present-day western Afghānistān. Rayy was the former capital of "Persian 'Irāq" and is now located south of Tehrān in Irān.

13 "Water and clay" is a symbol for the human body, as made by God. Although the people referred to here are not actual bodily and heredi-tary descendants of the Prophet and may speak Arabic, eastern Persian, or western Persian, they are still his spiritual descendants.

14 It is the same spiritual Reality and Light that guides all the prophets and saints of God.

15 This means that the Truth of what was revealed to Muhammad from God is an eternal "Sun" of spiritual meaning that is unchanged, despite the angle from which it is viewed.

It was his custom in *public* appearance and in secret *to pray*, "Guide my people,[8] for they do not know (the right way)."

The gates of both *this world and the next* are opened by means of his *interceding* words. *And* his prayer is answered in both worlds.

It is for this reason *that* he has been the Seal *of the Prophets*, that, in regard to his great generosity, there never was *any one* like him and there never will be.

Since in *the case of* a master *who* wins superiority in a skilled craft, don't you tell *him*, "This skilled craft is sealed on account of you"?

O *Muhammad*, in regard to opening seals, you are the Seal.[9] *And* in the world of the givers of the spirit, you are famous for generosity.

The intended meaning *here* is *that* the *spiritual* hints and indications *given by* Muhammad are entirely openings within openings, within openings.[10]

May a hundred thousand praises *be* upon his soul *and* on the arrival and epochs of his sons!

Those good-fortuned sons of his successors[11] are born from the root of his soul and heart.

If they are from Baghdād and Herāt or from Rayy,[12] they are his descendants without *any need of bodily* mixture of "water and clay."[13]

Wherever the *grafted* rose branch grows, it is the same rose *bush*,[14] wherever the jar of wine ferments, it is *from* the same *batch of* wine.

Even if the sun raises *its* head from the West,[15] it is the *same* identical sun, not something else.

(continued on page 161)

16 Rumi affirms that Muhammad was the greatest of the Prophets.

17 (Treasure) House of the Saints: The divinely inspired wisdom of the Prophet is the source of the illumination of the saints of Islam.

18 Rumi means himself here, as well as the Muslim saints and mystics (Sufis). It is necessary to follow the Qur'an and the model of the Prophet in order to receive full recognition and blessings from Sufi masters.

19 This refers to a saying of the Prophet: "My community is that community of believers which is blessed by (Divine) Mercy. Punishment will not (fall) upon them in the Hereafter. But its punishment will be in (this) world of temptation, misfortune, bloodshed, and tribulation." Muslims will not be punished at the Day of Judgment in the same way as peoples who rejected the Prophets sent by God.

20 "The way of conduct of Muhammad" refers to the model of his deeds and words [*sunnat*], which are an inspiration for his followers.

O Pride of the Prophets,[16] O *Treasure* House of the Saints,[17] and O Palace of *Special* Choosing! You are *our* Chief and other things *as well.*

∽∾

Our friend *is* youthful good fortune, *and* our work *is* giving *up* the soul. *And* Muhammad, the Pride of the World, is our caravan leader.

∽∾

Jesus *is* the comrade of Moses, *and* Jonas *is* the comrade of Joseph, *but* Muhammad sits alone, meaning, "I am distinct [*from other Prophets*]."

Love is the ocean of deep spiritual meaning, and everyone in the ocean is like a fish. *And* Muhammad is the pearl in the ocean. Look! I keep revealing *this.*

∽∾

Now, you should know that Muhammad is the leader and guide. As long as you don't come to Muhammad first, you won't reach us.[18]

∽∾

Be among the community *of believers* who are blessed by *Divine Mercy.*[19] Don't abandon the way of conduct of Muhammad,[20] *but* be commanded *by it.*

∽∾

(continued on page 163)

21 The spiritual influence of the Prophet continues in each generation and causes doubt, ignorance, unbelief, and polytheism to vanish (see *Nūr-i Muhammad* in the glossary).

22 Rumi refers to many different peoples becoming Muslims because of the enduring influence of the Light of Muhammad.

23 "Shadows": Religious creeds.

24 "And We have not sent you (O Muhammad) but (as) a bringer of good news and (as) a warner to all mankind, but most of mankind do not understand" (Q. 34:28). Rumi says elsewhere, "A star [of divine light] revealed its face in Muhammad, so that the substance [of the religion] of Jews and Zoroastrians passed away."

25 Here, Rumi was speaking about a Christian surgeon who asked him a question.

In regard to this newness *of the earth,* oldness is its opposite. *However,* that newness *of spiritual Reality* lacks opposite, resemblance, or number.

That *is* like the manner *in which* a hundred thousand kinds of darkness became luminous by means of the polishing *effects* of the Light of Muhammad.[21]

Among the Jews, polytheists, Christians, and Zoroastrians—all became a single color by that great hero.[22]

A hundred thousand short and long shadows[23] became one in the light of that mysterious Sun.

The Light of Muhammad does not abandon a Zoroastrian or Jew in the world.[24] May the shade of his good fortune shine upon everyone!

He brings all of those *who are* led astray into the Way out of the desert. May Muhammad be the guide on the Way of God forever!

Yes, it would be correct that *the Christian* should say,[25] "Truly the Lord of Jesus honored Jesus and brought him near *to His Presence.*" For the one who serves Jesus certainly serves the Lord, and the one who follows him certainly follows the Lord. But then God sent a more excellent Prophet than Jesus. He demonstrated by his hand what He demonstrated by the hand of Jesus. And more: it is obligatory that he should follow that Prophet of God Most High—*but* not for his sake. For one should not serve *anything* for itself except God, and one should not love *anything* for itself except God. And one loves *something* other than God *only* for the sake of God Most High, for truly the utmost goal is to your Lord. In other words, the limit is that you should love something for the sake of *something* other than it, until the extent that *you reach near* to God Most High, and love Him *only* for Himself.

(continued on page 165)

26 The Emigration, when the Prophet fled Mecca to live in Yathrib (later named Medina), marks the start of the Islamic calendar (in 621 C.E.).

27 If this date was meant to be specific, rather than general, it would have been two years before Rumi's death.

28 Bū Lahab was one of the Prophet's worst enemies, a polytheist who wished to eradicate the new monotheists.

29 That is, because of God-given kingly qualities within.

30 Rumi uses "kingship" to refer to the Muslim saints, or Sufis, who struggle for mastery of their passions in order to serve the Will of God.

Didn't Muhammad travel on a journey toward Medina?[26] He obtained dominion and became the king of a hundred countries.

Look at the existence of *the realm of* Muhammad. How enduring is it? It is strongly founded after six hundred and fifty years.[27]

Do you see anything *left* of the existence of *the Prophet's enemy* Bū Lahab and his kind?[28] Their story is remembered *only* for the sake of infamy and disgrace.

Since God willed that the religion of Muhammad should be greatly honoured and venerated, and apparent [to anyone], and to endure for ever.

The *real* king is the one who is a king from *within* himself.[29] He became a king not by *means of* treasuries and armies,

So that his kingship[30] continues forever, like the glory of the empire of the religion of Muhammad.

1 The Night Journey of the Prophet, who was taken up to Heaven by the angel Gabriel (see *Mi'rāj* in the glossary).

2 The Prophet Jesus is conceived as residing in the Heaven of the Sun. Muslims believe that the Prophet Jesus will return to earth as a sign of the imminent Day of Resurrection.

3 Muhammad's miraculous steed was said to be bigger than a donkey and smaller than a horse, and it bounded up into the Heavens in lightninglike flashes.

4 The direct experience of divine love is beyond the ability of the ordinary mind to understand with its thoughts, beliefs, and images.

5 In the Qur'an, the Prophet saw Gabriel "near the Lote Tree of the Utmost Limit" (53:14).

6 Gabriel told the Prophet (during the Ascension) that he could not travel closer to the Divine Throne or he would burn up.

20 □ The Night Journey, the Cave, and the Pillar

Muhammad has come back from the Ascension[1] *into the Heavens, and* Jesus has arrived from the Fourth Heaven.[2]

Did not Muhammad go on the Ascension at night? He took his miraculous steed[3] toward Heaven.

During the day *he was* in pursuit of accomplishments, *and* at night *he strove* for the sake of Love.

The people are sleeping, but the lovers are telling stories [*about their yearnings*] to God all night.

You will never arrive at *lofty spiritual* stations, like Muhammad, without the miraculous steed of Love and the striving of Gabriel.

In the noisy wind of Love, the intellect is *merely* a gnat—there is no place there for understanding and mind.[4]

Even the angel Gabriel drew *his* foot from *accompanying* Muhammad, when the journey was beyond the "Lote Tree."[5]

He said, "I will burn if I come *closer,*[6] since all is Love and annihilation in that direction."

(continued on page 169)

7 This line refers to the Prophet's Ascension (see *Mi'rāj* in the glossary) and his gazing toward the Divine Glory: "(Muhammad's) sight did not swerve nor turn away, for he certainly saw the greatest among the signs of his Lord" (Q. 53:17). This means, for the Sufis, that the Prophet never ceased gazing at the Presence of God during all his actions—an inspiring model for the mystics and lovers of God.

8 A popular Muslim belief that a verse in the Qur'an refers to a miracle done by the Prophet, who reportedly was with his companions one night when the moon appeared divided into two: "The Hour (of the coming Day of Judgment) is near and the moon was severed" (Q. 54:1). Rumi often uses this miracle as an image in his poetry.

9 The time for the Pilgrimage is during the lunar month called "Pilgrimage" [Hajj]. Since such months occur about ten days earlier in every solar year, the Pilgrimage season can be any time of the year, summer or winter.

10 Abu Bakr was the first, and closest, companion of the Prophet Muhammad. He became Muhammad's father-in-law (through the marriage of his daughter 'Āyisha) as well as his first successor. During the Prophet's flight from Mecca, he hid in a cave with Abu Bakr on the Emigration [Hijr] to Medina. By a miracle, the enemies who sought to kill the Prophet saw a spider's web covering the entrance of the cave, and they left. "For God did indeed help him when the unbelievers drove him out, he being the second of two when they were both in the cave, when he said to his companion, 'Fear not, for God is with us'" (Q. 9:40).

I "sewed" *my* two eyes *shut* from [*desires for*] this world and the next—
this I learned from Muhammad.

And the secret of "it did not swerve"[7] and "it did not turn away"—I
never could have learned *this* except from him.

Since you are among the family of the Prophet, come to the
Ascension. Since you are upon a high roof, kiss the moon's face.

Since he severed the moon,[8] why are you *remaining like* clouds? Since
he is active and quick-thinking, why are you lazy and confused?

When it is time for the Pilgrimage,[9] make *your* intention *to go to* the
Ka'ba; when you have gone *there, the city of* Mecca will also be seen *by you*.

For the intention *of the Prophet* during the *Heavenly* Ascension was the
vision of the Beloved; the Throne *of God* and the angels also appeared
following *that.*

Anyone may have a dear one or a companion.

Anyone may have a trade, and anyone *may have* a job.

But I am with the beloved's image and the furnace of the heart,
Like Muhammad and Abu Bakr in a corner of the cave.[10]

(*continued on page 171*)

11 According to stories about Rumi written within eighty years after his death, Rumi said, "Following (the example of) the Holy Prophet of God is among all the required duties for the people of spiritual reality."

12 A miracle story relates that a palm tree trunk used as a pillar in the Prophet's mosque made a groaning sound (expressing attachment to the Prophet) after it was replaced. (See chapter 10.)

13 See *Nūr-i Muhammad* in the glossary.

The generous one is like a fearful person *who* has gone into a chosen cave. The Sufi is hanging on to Muhammad,[11] like Abu Bakr.

I am *like* the pillar[12] of that mosque which the Prophet made a support. When he made another supporting beam *and replaced it*, I am groaning *also* from the pain of separation.

O Prophet of God! Regarding a pillar of patience, you made *it* a groaning beam in the end.

Similarly, if Muhammad doesn't make a path and support in my heart, perhaps I will lament *and* become *like* a groaning pillar.

The Light of Muhammad[13] soothed that groaning pillar, *so* don't be less than a piece of wood: be moaning, be moaning!

1 Rumi's interpretation is that the call to prayer, announced from the minarets of mosques, is the voice of the spirit of the Prophet inviting Muslims to follow his mode of prayer.

2 When Muslim mystics (Sufis) follow the Prophet's mode of prayer in the morning, they receive the blessings of his spiritual light and help.

3 "The mystical concert": Literally, "audition" [samā']. Ecstatic listening, chanting, moving, dancing, and whirling to spiritual poetry and music.

4 The ritual prayer is the formal Islamic prayer, which is obligatory for Muslims five times a day.

5 The meaning here is that the ecstasy of the Whirling Prayer in the Sufi master's presence is so blessed and holy that it resembles the blessing of someone who prayed behind the Prophet during his lifetime.

6 Glorifications are done individually and voluntarily, after the completion of any of the five daily ritual prayers, such as saying in Arabic thirty-three times each, "Glory be to God," "Praise be to God," and "God is Most Great."

7 This verse is spoken in one of Rumi's stories by a character who was complaining about the lack of authentic spirituality.

21 ☐ Prayer and Pilgrimage

Every morning *before dawn* the message of that Messenger of the beautiful ones arrives: "Come to prayer,[1] O helpless ones! *For* I am the remedy for the lovers *of God!*"[2]

You have been the way and the gate to the mystical concert[3] for the Heavens.

*And you've been the head and wings of the concert for the bird of the soul.

But in your presence, it is something else: *It is* like the *ritual* prayer[4] behind the Prophet![5]

Where is the Prophet's Path and his Companions? Where are his ritual prayer, *additional* glorifications *of God,*[6] and reverent and pious manners[7] [*now that they are needed*]?

(continued on page 175)

8 The House of God is the Ka'ba in Mecca, around which Muslims walk in a state of prayer. This is the place to which Muslim pilgrims travel on the Hajj and also the direction toward which all Muslims pray all over the world.

9 The majority of pilgrims also visit the Prophet's mosque and tomb in Medina, 280 miles north of Mecca, either prior to or following the completion of the Hajj rituals.

O *my* chief and lord, *who has* remained separated from your own town! [*Now is*] your joyous return from the journey to the House of God.[8]

Having spent days of the journey impoverished, *with* no rest *during* the nights, in the love of the Pilgrimage to the Ka'ba and the visit to *the grave of* Muhammad;[9]

Encrusted [*with dust on*] face and chest *while going* in that prayer direction [*established*] by God, *and* in the House of God *having* become truly *as the verse says*, "he was secure" (Q. 3:97).

1 This refers to the Sufi doctrine about the spiritual influence of the Prophet, which continues in each generation (see *Nūr-i Muhammad* in the glossary).

2 In the traditional Muslim state, the "People of the Book" (Christians and Jews) had a protected status (they could freely practice their own religion and enforce their own religious laws, were exempt from military service, and were to be protected from attack), in exchange for which they paid an annual tax. In addition, they wore a cord around the waist to identify them, which they broke off when converting to Islam.

3 Amazement is a mystical state of consciousness that transcends the ordinary mind and allows direct spiritual knowledge, certainty, and contemplation of divine attributes.

4 Rumi advises us to abandon our own limited opinions and follow the divinely inspired example of the Prophet. To the mystics, or Sufis, it means to transcend the limitations of the ordinary mind and to concentrate on being in the Presence of God alone. (It does not mean to avoid using reason and logic, which have their own place in Islam.)

5 A verse of the Qur'an reads, "Say: 'God is sufficient for me! Those who trust (rightly) place (their) trust upon Him'" (39:38; see also 9:129).

22 ☐ The Light of Muhammad and Intercession

The Light of Muhammad[1] has become a thousand branches (of knowledge), a thousand, *so that* both this world and the next have been seized from end to end.

If Muhammad rips the veil *open* from a single *such* branch, thousands of monks and priests will tear the string *of false belief from around their waists*.[2]

Sell *your* quick-thinking intellect and buy amazement,[3] *since* mental cleverness is *merely* conjecture and opinion, but amazement is *direct* vision [*of divine realities*].

Make *your* intellect a sacrifice[4] in the presence of Muhammad, *and* say, "'God is sufficient for me,'[5] since God is enough for *satisfying* me."

(*continued on page 179*)

6 God makes your soul radiant from the blessing of spiritual connection with the soul of the Prophet.

7 The sky was conceived as a series of concentric layers ascending to the Divine Throne.

8 This has become a title of the Prophet and is from a verse of the Qur'an in which God addressed Muhammad: "And We did not send you except as a mercy to (all) peoples" (21:107).

9 The Prophet ordered the destruction of the 360 idols that the Meccans kept inside the Ka'ba. For the Sufis, it is necessary to destroy inner "idols," such as pride and worldly desires.

10 The "idol" of the beloved refers to Shams-i Tabrīzī, Rumi's spiritual master, who represents the saint in whom personal attributes are annihilated and God's Attributes are reflected instead. It is a convention in Persian poetry for the beloved to be compared to an idol.

11 Rumi teaches not only that the Prophet will be the intercessor [shāfi'] for Muslim sinners on the Day of Judgment, but that his spirit can intercede with God for Muslims in this life (a belief that in our time is controversial).

12 This phrase refers to a verse of the Qur'an that praises the Prophet Muhammad during his Night Journey: "(His) sight did not swerve [from gazing at the Divine Presence], nor did it go astray" (53:17).

Sometimes He places a passion for silver, gold, and women within your nature. *And* sometimes He puts the radiance of the image of Muhammad[6] in your soul—

Drawing *you in* this direction toward bad and unpleasant people and *in* that direction drawing *you* toward good and delightful people. The ship will either pass *through safely* or break in these whirlpools.

Make many prayers secretly, wail much during the nights, so that the echo may come *back* into your ears from the dome of the seventh heaven.[7]

See *how* the good fortune of the dervishes *is* from "A mercy to *all* peoples,"[8] *so that their* cloaks *are* like the shining *full* moon *and their* shawls *are* like the fragrant rose.

We broke many idols in the presence of Muhammad,[9] until we reached *our* heart's desire in the "idol" of the beloved.[10]

For that *reason*, Muhammad was the intercessor[11] for every scar of *shame*, since his eyes "did not swerve"[12] from *anyone* except the King.

(continued on page 181)

13 Rumi viewed Shams-i Tabrīzī as merged with the guiding spirit of the Prophet Muhammad, as is shown in the *Dīvān*, where Rumi sometimes mentions the Prophet and Shams in the same verse.

O brightness *and* direction[13] of those who seek help from the spirit of Muhammad!

Muhammad did not come "except as a mercy to *all* peoples."

He brings those who have lost the way from the desert to the Way: may Muhammad be *our* guardian upon the Way of God eternally!

1 Medina is the city in present-day Saudi Arabia where the Prophet is buried, in the location of his house next to his mosque.

2 These words from the Qur'an describe Paradise: "Truly the righteous and pious will be in (a place abounding with) gardens and rivers, in a resting place of Truth, in the presence of an All-Powerful King" (Q. 54:55).

3 Rumi refers to the famous "Light Verse" of the Qur'an, involving a parable of divine light in which a lamp is described as "ignited from a blessed tree, an olive (tree which is) not of the East and not of the West" (Q. 24:35).

4 The black clothes symbolize here a state of mourning, meaning that unbelief—the denial of the Existence, Oneness, and Will of God—will be defeated.

5 This refers to the spiritual influence of the Prophet, which continues in each generation (see *Nūr-i Muhammad* in the glossary).

23 □ Death and Resurrection

Those *bodily* senses in Muhammad which are transient are asleep at this time beneath the earth of Medina.[1]

But that magnificent nature of his, which is brave and heroic, is unchanged and uncorrupted in "a resting place of Truth."[2]

The qualities of the body are *in* the place of corruptible things, *but* the enduring spirit is a radiant sun,

Lacking corruption, since it is "not of the West," *and* lacking change, since it is "not of the East."[3]

The sun never became faint from awe of a mote *of dust*, nor did a candle ever become unconscious by *the presence of* a moth.

The body of Muhammad *is* dependent upon that *corruption. But* know that this change and corruption is *only* the property of the body,

Such as illness, sleep, and suffering—*whereas* the spirit is pure and isolated from these qualities.

∽

When Muhammad's form passed away, *the proclamation of* "God is Most Great" seized the world.

∽

Unbelief put on black clothes[4] *and* the light of Muhammad[5] arrived. The Drum of Eternity was beaten *and* the eternal Kingdom arrived.

(continued on page 185)

6 An astrolabe is an astronomical instrument used for studying the planets and stars.

7 The seven heavens are the orbital areas of the sky "governed" by the "wandering stars" in layers of distance from earth, according to ancient Ptolemaic astronomy: Moon, Mercury, Venus, Sun, Mars, Jupiter, and Saturn.

8 Here, Rumi envisions the "explanation" of the hearts of all the Muslim Sufi saints and masters as contained in seven volumes. In contrast to the thousands of books written on Islamic law, Islamic mysticism is based on direct knowledge of God within the heart.

The heart was like an astrolabe[6] *and became* the sign of the seven Heavens.[7] *Then* the explanation of the heart of a Muhammad arrived in seven volumes.[8]

Notes □

Introduction

1. A. J. Arberry, "Discourses of Rumi," p. 9.
2. First translated by Nicholson, 1898, *Selected Poems from the Dīvāni Shamsi Tabrīz*, no. XXXI, p. 125. This poem does not occur in the earliest manuscripts of Rumi's *Dīvān* and is no longer considered to be authentic by scholars. Nicholson found this poem in only one manuscript used by him (dated 170 years after Rumi died).
3. First translated by Nicholson, 1898, no. XVII, pp. 71–73. This poem also does not occur in the earliest manuscripts of the *Dīvān* and is no longer considered to be authentic by scholars. Nicholson mentioned that this poem occurred in only one manuscript (dated more than 170 years after Rumi died).
4. This quatrain does not exist in the earliest manuscripts of Rumi's *Dīvān*, but is found in manuscripts of a contemporary poet, Bābā Afzaluddīn Kāshānī (died 1274); it has long been attributed to Abu Saʿīd ibn Abi 'l-Khayr (died 1048), for which see Abramian, *Nobody, Son of Nobody: Poems of Shaikh Abu Saeed Abil Kheir* (Prescott, Arizona: Hohm Press, 2001), p. 4.
5. *Mathnawi*, Book II: 1757–59, Persian edition, using the verse numbers of the text edited by R. A. Nicholson, 1926–34.
6. Dr. Ravan Farhadi, an Afghan scholar, has pointed out that references to "Hindus" in Rumi's poetry often refer to Indian Muslims. By this time, Islam had been established in India for over five hundred years (since 712 C.E.). It was spread further, especially by the Ghaznavid Sultan Mahmūd (died 1030), whose kingdom was called "the dominion of Hind and Sind" by a famous Persian Sufi master (Ahmad Ghazzālī, died 1126, in his book *Sawānih*, chapt. 39). By 1206 (a year before Rumi's birth), the sultanate of Delhi had been established. An example of a reference to Indian Muslims is Rumi's well-known story of the elephant

186

brought from India for display (to a people unfamiliar with the animal) and kept in a dark house by "Hindus" (*Hunūd*, the Arabic plural of "Hindu"—*Math.* Book III: 1259). Rumi also uses the term "Hendū" to mean a dark-skinned slave (as in *Math.* Book III: 2839), as well as a metaphor for beautiful and intensely black eyes or hair, as in the verse, "O Turk, why are you with Indian [*Henduwiy*] curls?" (Quatrain No. 1978). The term "Hendū" in the Persian of Rumi's time, according to Dr. Farhadi, meant the peoples along the Indus River. Those who worshipped according to the native Indian religion were called "Henduwān-i mushrik" (Hindu idolators). Only much later did the term "Hendū" come to mean in Persian a worshipper of the Hindu faith.

7. *Math.*, Book II: 1770.

8. *Math.*, Book VI: 233.

9. There are several poems in Rumi's Dīvān which contain a mixture of Persian and Greek. See Franklin Lewis, *Rumi: Past and Present, East and West*, p. 316.

10. *Fīhi Mā Fīhi*, Discourse No. 29.

11. *Fīhi Mā Fīhi*, Discourse No. 20.

12. Aflākī, "The Glorious Talents and Abilities of the Knowers of God" (*Manāqibu 'l-'arifīn*), Chapter 3, section 450.

13. Aflākī, "The Glorious Talents and Abilities of the Knowers of God" (*Manāqibu 'l-'ārifīn*), Chapter 3, section 290.

14. A. J. Arberry, "Discourses of Rumi," p. 4.

15. Aflākī, "The Glorious Talents and Abilities of the Knowers of God" (*Manāqibu 'l-'ārifīn*), Chapter 3, sections 207, 539.

16. Aflākī, "The Glorious Talents and Abilities of the Knowers of God" (*Manāqibu 'l-'ārifīn*), Chapter 8, section 51.

17. Aflākī, "The Glorious Talents and Abilities of the Knowers of God" (*Manāqibu 'l-'ārifīn*), Chapter 3, section 580.

18. Aflākī, "The Glorious Talents and Abilities of the Knowers of God" (*Manāqibu 'l-'ārifīn*), Chapter 3, section 505.

19. *Math*, Book I: 3504. See Chapter 12 and note 2.

20. The specific words are translated by Franklin Lewis (in an extensive chapter with new information in English about Shams-i Tabrīzī, *Rumi—Past and Present, East and West*, p. 150; also translated by O'Kane, *The Feats of the Knowers of God*, p. 468.

21. Aflākī, "The Glorious Talents and Abilities of the Knowers of God (*Manāqibu 'l-'ārifīn*), Chapter 6, section 14, p. 759; also translated by O'Kane,*The Feats of the Knowers of God*, p. 530.

22. *Math.*, Book I, Preface.

23. Anqaravi, *Sharh-i Kabīr-i Anqaravī bar Masnavī*, translated into Persian by 'Ismat Sattārzāda, in 15 volumes, 1970. A seventeenth-century Ottoman Turkish commentary.

Chapter 1

1. "The greatest warfare": Arabic text in Anqaravi, *Sharh-i Kabīr-i Anqaravī bar Masnavī*, Vol. 2, p. 569.

   "Your worst enemy": Arabic text in Forūzānfar, *Ahādīs-i Masnavī*, no. 17, p. 9; transliteration of Arabic text in Nicholson, *The Mathnawī of Jalālu'ddīn Rūmī*, Vol. 7, "Commentary on Book I," p. 76.

   "Truly the one who overcomes his cravings": In Forūzānfar, *Ahādīs-i Masnavī*, no. 37, pp. 16–17.

6. "Enough, enough": In Nicholson, *The Mathnawī of Jalālu'ddīn Rūmī*, Vol. 7, "Commentary on Book I," p. 103; in Anqaravi, *Sharh-i Kabīr-i Anqaravī bar Masnavī*, Vol. 2, p. 570.

Chapter 2

4. "Our Lord was amazed": In Forūzānfar, *Ahādīs-i Masnavī*, no. 305, p. 103.
6. "In this condition of fetters and chains": *Fīhi Mā Fīhi*, Discourse No. 12.
8. "One night the Prophet felt pain in his hands": *Fīhi Mā Fīhi*, Discourse No. 15.

Chapter 3

4. "Piety is worshiping God": In Nurbaksh, "Traditions of the Prophet," Vol. I, pp. 64–65; in Nicholson, Vol. 7, "Commentary on Book II," p. 284, and "Commentary on Book I," p. 191.

5. "My Companions are like the stars": In Forūzānfar, *Ahādīth-i Mathnawī*, no. 86, p. 35 and no. 44, p. 19; in *Anqaravi, Sharh-i Kabīr*, Vol. 3, p. 1326; in Nicholson, Vol. 7, "Commentary on Book I," p. 180.

15. "Because commonality is a wonderful attractor": *Math.*, Book IV: 2671–72.

Chapter 4

3. This story of Muhammad's visit to the sick man is mentioned in Nicholson, Vol. 7, "Commentary on Book II," p. 315; in *Anqaravi, Sharh-i Kabīr*, Vol. 5, p. 860, as derived from the famous collection of *Ahādīth* named *Sahīh al-Muslim*.

11. "The (helping) Hand of God": In *Anqaravi, Sharh-i Kabīr*, Vol. 5, p. 742.

13. "The one who wants to sit together with God": In Forūzānfar, *Ahādīs-i Masnavī*, no. 635, p. 198; in Nurbakhsh, "Traditions of the Prophet," Vol. 2, p. 57; see *Math.* I: 1529 (heading); VI: 1302. The word *Sūfī* did not come into use until some time after the Prophet's death.

Chapter 5

4. "O Bilāl, revive us": In Forūzānfar, *Ahādīs-i Masnavī*, no. 48, p. 21.

11. "The prayer of someone (who is) absent": In Anqaravi, *Sharh-i Kabīr-i Anqaravī bar Masnavī*, Vol. 7, p. 97.

Chapter 6

1. "A caravan of Arabs": This miracle story about the Prophet has been retold in *Nuzhatu 'l-Nāzirīn* (in Arabic) by Al-Maqdisī, died 1624 c.e. (Nicholson, Vol. 8, "Commentary on Book III," p. 81; *Sharh-i Anqaravi bar Masnavi*, Vol. 8, p. 1219.

10. "Truly,...My Mercy precedes My wrath": *Sahīh al-Bukhār*, Vol. 9, pp. 482, 483; Forūzānfar, *Ahādīth-i Mathnawī*, no. 46, p. 26, & no. 468, p. 152.

Chapter 7

4. "The unbeliever eats": In Forūzānfar, *Ahādīth-i Mathnawī*, no. 449, p. 145.

35. "So increase (your) need": *Math.*, Book II: 3280.

40. "God says": In Forūzānfar, *Ahādīs-i Masnavī*, no. 264, pp. 93–94; in Nicholson, Vol. 7, "Commentary on Book I," p. 28.

Chapter 8

6. "Men are (like) mines": In Forūzānfar, *Ahādīs-i Masnavī*, no. 159, pp. 61–62; in Nicholson, Vol. 7, "Commentary on Book II," p. 313.

Chapter 10

2. This story is in *Anqaravi, Sharh-i Kabīr*, Vol. 3, p. 835; in Nicholson, Vol. 7, "Commentary on Book I," p. 141.

7. "The (skeptical) philosopher": *Math.*, Book I: 3278; "For you, the (groaning) pillar": *Math.*, Book VI: 858.

Chapter 11

18. "If not for the foolishness": In Forūzānfar, *Ahādīs-i Masnavī*, no. 339, p. 113; in Nicholson, *The Mathnawī of Jalālu'ddīn Rūmī*, Vol. 7, "Commentary on Book I," p. 139; "God placed a seal upon their eyes and mouths": *Math.*, Book IV: 669–70.

Chapter 12

1. This story is in *Anqaravi, Sharh-i Kabīr,* Vol. 3, pp. 1271–72; in Nicholson, Vol. 7, "Commentary on Vol. 1," pp. 204–05, where he states that this is known as the "Tradition about Hārithah" (whom Rumi changed to another person in the Prophet's life, Zayd); in Lewis, *Rumi: Past and Present, East and West,* p. 290.

10. "The fortunate and blessed person": In Forūzānfar, *Ahādīs-i Masnavī,* no. 84, p. 35.

30. "If desire were to leap up": *Math.,* Book II: 572–73.

32. "See the (Holy) Mountain": Ode No. 1311, line 13878.

39. "Those rivers (in Paradise)": *Math.,* Book III: 3468.

Chapter 13

1. "My eyes are sleeping": In Forūzānfar, *Ahādīs-i Masnavī,* no. 188, pp. 69–70; in *Anqaravi, Sharh-i Kabīr,* Vol. 6, p. 1175; in Nicholson, Vol. 7, "Commentary on Book II," p. 361; see *Math.* III: 1226.

3. "I have a time with God": In Forūzānfar, *Ahādīs-i Masnavī,* no. 39, p. 17; in Forūzānfar, *Kolliyāt-i Shams,* Vol. 3, p. 186.

4. "My Lord gives me food": In Forūzānfar, *Ahādīs-i Masnavī,* no. 89, p. 36; in Nicholson, Vol. 7, "Commentary on Book I," p. 214; see also *Math.* Book I: 3740.

8. "No ritual prayer is complete": In Forūzānfar, *Ahādīs-i Masnavī,* no. 10, p. 5; in Nicholson, Vol. 7, "Commentary on Book I," p. 39.

9. "O God, show us the true as the true": In Forūzānfar, *Ahādīs-i Masnavī,* no. 351, p. 116; in *Anqaravi, Sharh-i Kabīr,* Vol. 15, p. 1078; in Nicholson, Vol. 7, "Commentary on Book I," p. 164.

11. "O God, show us things": In Forūzānfar, *Ahādīs-i Masnavī,* no. 116, p. 45; in Forūzānfar, *Kolliyāt-i Shams,* Vol. 7, p. 102; in Nicholson, Vol. 7, "Commentary on Book II," p. 254.

13. "Truly I seek the forgiveness of God": In Forūzānfar, no. 425, pp. 138–39; in *Anqaravi, Sharh-i Kabīr,* Vol. 11, p. 1212; in Nicholson, "Commentary on Book IV," p. 206.

19. "The (true) believer is discerning": In Forūzānfar, *Ahādīs-i Masnavī,* no. 178, p. 67.

20. "The (true) believer sees by the Light of God": In Forūzānfar, *Ahādīs-i Masnavī,* no. 33, p. 14.

22. "The parable of my (religious) community": In Forūzānfar, *Ahādīs-i Masnavī,* no. 334, p. 111.

24. "The elder among his followers": In Forūzānfar, *Ahādīs-i Masnavī,* no. 224, p. 82; in *Anqaravi, Sharh-i Kabīr,* Vol. 10, p. 219. See also *Math.* Book IV: 1774.

27. "The one who makes (his) cares": In Forūzānfar, Ahādīs-i Masnavī, no. 415, p. 136; "Whoever chooses care for religion": Math., Book IV: 3137; see also Book V: 1084, Heading.

31. "(For) it may be that a breath": In Forūzānfar, Ahādīs-i Masnavī, no. 46, p. 20.

37. "I am the final": In Forūzānfar, Ahādīs-i Masnavī, no. 181, pp. 67–68; in Anqaravi, Sharh-i Kabīr, Vol. 6, p. 1012; see also Math., Book III: 1128–9, Book IV: 525–29, Fīhi Mā Fīhi, Discourse No. 49.

Chapter 14

1. "The (true) believer is like the lute": In Forūzānfar, Kolliyāt-i Shams, Vol. 3, p. 58; in Forūzānfar, Kolliyāt-i Shams, Vol. 7, p. 95; in Nicholson, Vol. 8, "Commentary on Book VI," p. 394.

2. "Were made swollen": In Forūzānfar, Kolliyāt-i Shams, Vol. 7, p. 95.

4. "Whatever God wills": In Forūzānfar, Ahādīs-i Masnavī, no. 554, p. 174.

6. "My satan has submitted": In Forūzānfar, Kolliyāt-i Shams, Vol. 1, p. 56, Vol. 2, p. 79; in Schimmel, Mystical Dimensions of Islam, p. 115.

10. "Die before death": In Forūzānfar, Ahādīs-i Masnavī, no. 352, p. 116; cited in Nicholson, Vol. 8, "Commentary on Book IV," p. 183; see also Math. Book VI: 754–55; Book V: 602–7.

11. "A dead one who is living": In Forūzānfar, Ahādīs-i Masnavī, no. 616, pp. 193–94; cited by Nicholson, Vol. 8, "Commentary on Book VI," p. 326.

13. "Poverty is my pride": In Forūzānfar, Ahādīs-i Masnavī, no. 45, p. 23.

15. "The one who has known himself": In Forūzānfar, Ahādīs-i Masnavī, no. 529, pp. 166–67; in Anqaravi, Sharh-i Kabīr, Vol. 13, p. 787.

Chapter 15

1. "My earth does not contain Me": In Forūzānfar, Ahādīs-i Masnavī, no. 63, pp. 25–26; in Anqaravi, Sharh-i Kabır, Vol. 3, p. 1012; in Nicholson, Vol. 7, Vol. 7, "Commentary on Book I," p. 167.

3. "I was a Hidden Treasure": In Forūzānfar, Ahādīs-i Masnavī, no. 70, pp. 28–29; in Forūzānfar, Kolliyāt-i Shams, Vol. 7, p. 137; see Math. Book VI: 1659–61.

4. "If not for you": In Forūzānfar, Ahādīs-i Masnavī, no. 546, p. 172, and no. 655, p. 203; in Forūzānfar, Kolliyāt-i Shams, Vol. 3, p. 49; in Anqaravi, Sharh-i Kabīr, Vol. 13, p. 874; in Nicholson, Vol. 7, "Commentary on Book I," p. 55, and in "Commentary on Book II," p. 275.

Chapter 16

8. "It has been said of Rumi": In Aflākī, "The Glorious Talents and Abilities of the Knowers of God" *(Manāqibu 'l-'ārifīn)*, Chapter 3, section 353.

Chapter 17

1. The ode appears in "Mevlevi Ayinleri," edited by Sadettin Heper (Konya, Turkey: Konya Turizm Dernegi Yayini, 1979); in Schimmel, "And Muhammad Is His Messenger," p. 306. However, this ode is not in the earliest manuscripts of Rumi's *Dīvān* as edited by the Iranian scholar Forūzānfar.

Chapter 19

11. "His successors": See the saying of the Prophet, "I am from the Light of God and the true believers are from me," cited by Nicholson, Vol. 8, "Commentary on Book VI," p. 315. In another Tradition [*Hadīth*], the Prophet said, "The mercy of God is upon my successors." When his companions asked the meaning of this, he explained, "Those who love my way of conduct [*sunnat*] and know the servants of God," cited by Anqaravi, *Anqaravi, Sharh-i Kabīr*, Vol. 14, p. 74.

19. "My community": In Anqaravi, Vol. 14, p. 158; in Nicholson, Vol. 7, "Commentary on Book I," p. 188.

24. "A star [of divine light]": *Math.*, Book V: 3397.

Chapter 20

6. "Or he would burn up": In Forūzānfar, editor, *Kolliyāt-i Shams*, Vol. 2, p. 107.

11. "Following (the example of) the Holy Prophet of God": quoted in Aflākī, "The Glorious Talents and Abilities of the Knowers of God *(Manāqibu 'l-'ārifīn)*, Chapter 3, section 154, p. 242.

dervish: The Turkish spelling of a Persian word [*darvīsh*], which means "poor one," in the sense of someone who is humble before God, who is "the All-Rich" (Q. 35:15). It is also the name for a Sufi, or practitioner of Islamic mysticism.

dhikru 'llāh: Remembrance of God. This consists of reading the Qur'an (known as the Reminder), as well as being mindful and conscious of the Presence of God throughout the day. Among Muslim mystics, or Sufis, this also consists of chanting (out loud or silently, in a group or individually) the praises of God, using Arabic terms and phrases from the Holy Qur'an.

faqīr (pronounced "faqeer"): "Poor one" in Arabic, and translated into Persian as *darvīsh*.

Hadīth (pronounced "Hadeeth"; the plural is *Ahādīth*): Something related about what the Prophet Muhammad said or did.

Hanafī: A school of Islamic law (founded by Imām Abu Hanīfa, who died about 500 years before Rumi, part of the Sunnī branch of Islam, and the tradition of daily Islamic conduct followed by Rumi.

Hijrah: The Migration of the Prophet from (the Arabian city of) Mecca, where he was born and raised, to Medina in the year 622 c.e., the start of the Muslim calendar.

Īmān: (True) faith, defined in Islam as affirming the truths that there is no god but (the One True) God and that Muhammad is the Prophet of God; that God has divine attributes as the sole Creator and Ruler of the universe who is Unique, All-Knowing, All-Powerful, All-Present, All-Providing, All-Loving, Perfectly Just, and so on; that what God Wills to be is Destined to occur, but individuals should strive their utmost to do good works;

that Angels exist; that Revelations given to Prophets from God have become revealed scriptures; that there is a Hereafter involving the Resurrection and Day of Judgment, that the pious and righteous will be rewarded with Paradise, but the rejecting wrongdoers will be punished with Hell—except as God wills, and depending on Divine Mercy and Forgiveness.

Islam: "Submission" to the Will of the One God. This is the essential message of all true Prophets, from Noah and Abraham to Moses, Jesus, and Muhammad. It also includes the worship of no divinity except the One God and Creator of the Heavens and the earth, and belief in divine justice on the Day of Judgment.

jihād: Striving, struggle, making effort. Physical combat in defense against invaders or oppressors is only one form of "striving for the sake of God." In Islamic mysticism, a priority is placed on combating the base ego with its cravings, ambitions, pride, and so on.

Ka'ba: The cube-shaped building in Mecca, Saudi Arabia, the direction toward which all Muslims in the world face to pray. It is empty (containing only some lamps and a ladder to the roof), and is believed to have been originally built by the Prophet Abraham as the first temple devoted to the worship of One God.

kāfir: An unbeliever, one who denies the One True God (such as worshiping other deities or partners along with God, who is Unique), who is ungrateful to God for the abundance and blessings of the creation, and who rejects the authority of God's Messengers and Prophets—from Noah and Abraham, to Moses, Jesus, and Muhammad.

Khalīfa: The representative, or vice-regent, of God on earth. This term refers to the creation of mankind by God as His vice-regent on earth (Q. 2:30) prior to the fall of Adam and Eve from Paradise. It also means any of the Prophets of God, especially those who exercised authority. In Sufism, it means an appointed representative or successor of a Muslim spiritual master. In political terms, the term is used to mean the ruler of the Islamic state (the Caliph), as a "successor" of the Prophet Muhammad who ruled the first Islamic state. The last Caliphate ended in 1922, following the collapse of the Ottoman Empire after being defeated in World War I and the founding of the Turkish Republic.

Mathnawī (also *Masnavi, Mesnevi, Mathnavi*): A word meaning "rhymed couplets," it is also the name of Rumi's masterpiece of stories and Islamic wisdom, interpreted from a mystical (Sufi) viewpoint.

Mawlānā (also *Maulana; Mevlana* in Turkey): "our Master." This name, traditionally given to religious scholars, most notably refers to Mawlana Jalaluddin Rumi.

Mevlevi: The Turkish spelling of *Mawlawī* (*"Mōlavī"* in Persian), which means "having to do with the Master," Mawlana Jalaluddin Rumi. It refers to the order of Islamic mysticism (Sufism) that maintains the teachings and spiritual practices of Rumi and his successors. The Mevlevi order formerly had numerous centers throughout the Ottoman Empire, but has been struggling to survive since 1925, when organized Sufism was made illegal in Turkey (and remains so).

Mi'rāj: The (Heavenly) Ascension, the famous Night Journey in which the Prophet was brought by the angel Gabriel to the site of the former Temple of Jerusalem (see Q. 94:1; 20:25) and then into the Heavens, where he met the souls of previous Prophets and the angels, saw many heavenly sights, and was guided up to the Divine Throne.

mosque: A word that came into the French language and then into English, derived from the Arabic word *masjid* (place of prayers of prostration).

Muhammad: The Prophet to whom was given the Islamic Revelation in the seventh century C.E., the scriptures called the Holy Qur'an, in the Arabic language. Rumi usually calls him by the honorific titles *Mustafā* (the "Chosen" Prophet of God) and *Ahmad* (an intensification of the name *Muhammad,* meaning "most praiseworthy"). Both of these epithets are rendered in this book as *Muhammad.*

mu'min: A true believer, one who believes and worships the Creator as One God who has no partners, sons, or daughters and who accepts the authority of the revelations of the Prophets—the last of which was through the Prophet Muhammad. It is also a Name of God, the Most Faithful, the source of all true faith.

Muslim: One who submits to the divine will, following the way of surrender [*islām*] taught by the Holy Qur'an and the Prophet Muhammad, and who is rewarded by God with peace and security [*salām*].

nafs: Literally, "self." The base ego, which includes the bodily or "animal" self with its cravings, negative emotions, the opinionated and prideful mind, as well as the illusion of separate selfhood that leads to "worshiping" the "idol" of self instead of God and obeying self-will instead of God's Will.

Nūr-i Muhammad: Light of Muhammad, the spiritual blessing that guided all of the Prophets through the final one, Muhammad, and that continues to guide the Sufi saints and masters, the Muslim community, and humanity as a whole.

qibla: The prayer direction toward Mecca (and the Ka'ba), which a Muslim faces when doing the five daily ritual prayers.

Qur'an: Literally, "recitation." The name for the Revelation given by God to the Prophet Muhammad, through the angel Gabriel. It consists of 114 chapters in Arabic.

samā': Literally, "audition," translated here as "mystical concert." Ecstatic listening, chanting, singing, moving, and dancing or whirling to spiritual poetry and music. The use of musical instruments in religious gatherings is generally condemned in Islam as a blameworthy innovation. Still, it has been practiced in a few Sufi orders as a praiseworthy innovation that may increase the piety of some (carefully selected) participants.

Shāfi'ī: One of the four major schools of Sunnī Islamic law, and the one that was followed by Shams-i Tabrīzī.

shahādat: The Testimony of Faith, repeated by all Muslims in each of the five daily ritual prayers, announced in the call to prayer that precedes such prayers done in congregation, and said in the presence of Muslim witnesses by anyone who decides to convert to Islam. The Testimony is: "I bear witness that there is no divinity except (the One) God. And I bear witness that Muhammad is His slave and His messenger."

Sharī'at: The Religious Law of Islam, derived from the Holy Qur'an and from the sacred Traditions [*Ahādīth*] based on the sayings and doings of the Prophet.

shaykh (also *shaikh* or *sheikh*): Literally, "old man," a spiritual master or guide in Sufism.

Sūfī (pronounced "Soofee"): A practitioner of Islamic mysticism, or Sufism, who seeks to surrender to the divine will to a profound degree.

Sufism: The English word for the "Sufi way" [*tasawwuf*], which is based on the foundation of daily Islamic practices, involves the purification of the soul from worldly cravings in order to develop virtues pleasing to God, and aspires to a profound level of surrender to the Will and Glory of God so that ordinary self-centered thoughts and desires may no longer dominate and one may become a true servant of God in speech and actions. It may also be called Islamic mysticism, or the Islamic path to transcendence of the illusions of distinctions and separations maintained by the ordinary mind, and to direct realization of the transcendent Oneness of the Creator: "Whichever way you turn, there is the Face of God" (Q. 2:115).

Sunnat: The way of conduct of the Prophet, the model of his deeds and words, which are an inspiration for his followers.

Sunnī (also spelled "Sunnite"): The majority branch of Islam (more than 85 percent), which is distinct from the Shī'ī (or Shi'ite) branch of Islam. In Rumi's time, most Persian-speaking Muslims were part of the Sunnī branch. It was not until the sixteenth century that Shī'ī Islam became predominant in Persia (now called Iran).

Suggested Readings and Resources ☐

Translations of the Mathnawi

Arberry, Arthur J., translator. *Tales from the Masnavi*. London: George Allen & Unwin, 1961. A British prose translation of the major stories, with Rumi's digressions deleted.

———. *More Tales from the Masnavi*. London: George Allen & Unwin, 1963.

Chittick, William C., translator. *The Sufi Path of Love: The Spiritual Teachings of Rumi*. Albany: State University of New York Press, 1983. A compilation of quotations from Rumi's works arranged very usefully into major themes and translated into very clear American English.

Nicholson, Reynold A., translator. *The Mathnawī of Jalālu'ddīn Rūmī*. Containing the translation in three volumes. London: Cambridge University Press, 1926, 1930, 1934 (reprinted since). A British translation of the complete text.

———. *Tales of Mystic Meaning*. London: 1931 (reprinted, Oxford: Oneworld, 1995). A short selection from his complete translation of the *Mathnawi*.

Türkmen, Erkan, translator. *The Essence of Rumi's Masnevi: Including His Life and Works*. Konya, Turkey: Eris Booksellers, 1992. Excellent selections translated together with brief commentaries.

Whinfield, E. H., translator. *Masnavi i Ma'navi: Teachings of Rumi, The Spiritual Couplets of Maulāna Jalālu-'d-dīn Muhammad i Rūmī*. London, 1887. Reprinted. London: Octagon Press, 1979. An abridged translation.

Interpretive Versions of the Mathnawi Based on Nicholson's Translation

Barks, Coleman. *The Soul of Rumi: A New Collection of Ecstatic Poems*. New York: HarperCollins, 2001. Concludes with over one hundred pages of condensed poetic interpretations from Book IV of the *Mathnawi* (based also on translations by the Indian scholar M. G. Gupta).

Helminski, Camille, and Kabir Helminski. *Rumi: Daylight: A Daybook of Spiritual Guidance: Three Hundred and Sixty-Five Selections from Jelaluddin Rumi's Mathnawi*. Putney, Vt.: Threshold Books, 1994. Short excerpts conscientiously rendered into American English.

———. *Jewels of Remembrance: A Daybook of Spiritual Guidance Containing Three Hundred and Sixty-Five Selections from the Wisdom of Rumi*. Putney, Vt.: Threshold Books, 1996.

Scholey, Arthur. *The Paragon Parrot and Other Inspirational Tales of Wisdom: Rumi Retold by Arthur Scholey*. London: Watkins Publishing, 2002. A short selection of summarized stories.

Works about the Mathnawi

Chittick, William C. *The Sufi Doctrine of Rumi: An Introduction*. Tehran: Aryamehr University, 1974.

Hakim, Khalifa 'Abdul. *The Metaphysics of Rumi*. Lahore: Institute of Islamic Culture, 1965.

Iqbal, Afzal. *The Life and Work of Muhammad Jalal-ud-Din Rumi*, 3rd rev. ed. Lahore: Institute of Islamic Culture, 1974.

Khosla, K. *The Sufism of Rumi*. Great Britain: Element Books, 1987.

Nicholson, Reynold A. *The Mathnawī of Jalālu'ddīn Rūmī*. Containing the commentary in two volumes. London: Cambridge University Press, 1937, 1940. A valuable contribution to understanding the text (verse numbers are in Arabic).

Renard, John. *All the King's Falcons: Rumi on Prophets and Revelation*. Albany: State University of New York Press, 1994. Revised from a doctoral dissertation on Rumi's teachings on the Prophets mentioned in the Qur'an, including Muhammad.

Schimmel, Annemarie. *I Am Wind You Are Fire: The Life and Work of Rumi*. Boston: Shambhala, 1992.

———. *The Triumphal Sun: A Study of the Works of Jalaloddin Rumi*. London: Fine Books, 1978.

Other Works

Asad, Muhammad, translator. *The Message of the Qur'ān: Translated and Explained*. Gibraltar: Dar Al-Andalus, 1980, 1984. The most suitable translation for Westerners, with excellent commentary.

A. Yusuf Ali, translator. *The Holy Qur'ān: Text, Translation and Commentary*. Washington, D.C.: McGregor & Werner, 1946. An excellent translation with helpful commentary.

Arberry, Arthur J., translator. *Discourses of Rumi*. London: John Murray, 1961. The first complete translation into English of Rumi's *Fīhi Mā Fīhi*.

———. *Mystical Poems of Rumi*. Chicago: University of Chicago Press, 1968. Accurate translations of odes from Rumi's *Dīvān*, in British English.

————. *Mystical Poems of Rumi: Second Selection.* Boulder, Colo.: Westview Press, 1979.

Chittick, William C. *Sufism: A Short Introduction.* Oxford: Oneworld, 2000.

Ernst, Carl. *The Shambhala Guide to Sufism.* Boston: Shambhala, 1997.

Fadiman, James, and Robert Frager, eds. *Essential Sufism.* San Francisco: Harper-Collins, 1997.

Farhadi, A.G. Ravan, translator. *Abdullah Ansari of Herat: An Early Sufi Master.* Surrey, Great Britain: Curzon, 1996.

Frager, Robert. *The Wisdom of Islam: A Practical Guide to the Wisdom of Islamic Belief.* Hauppauge, N.Y.: Barrons, 2002.

Glassé, Cyril. *The Concise Encyclopedia of Islam.* San Francisco: HarperSanFrancisco, 1989.

Lewis, Franklin D. *Rumi: Past and Present, East and West—The Life, Teachings and Poetry of Jalāl al-Din Rumi.* Oxford: Oneworld, 2000, rev. ed. 2003. A comprehensive study of Rumi's influence, with much new material that clarifies his life and teachings.

Nasr, Seyyed Hossein. *Muhammad: Man of Allah.* London: Muhammadi Trust of Britain and Northern Ireland, 1982.

Nurbakhsh, Javad, editor. *Traditions of the Prophet* Volume 1. New York: Khaniqahi-Nimatullahi Publications, 1981.

————. *Traditions of the Prophet* Volume 2. New York: Khaniqahi-Nimatullahi Publications, 1983.

O'Kane, John, translator. *Shams al-Din Ahmad-e Aflākī: The Feats of the Knowers of God* (Manāqeb al-'ārefīn). Boston: Brill, 2002. The first complete translation into English of accounts (including many miracle stories) of Rumi's sayings and doings (collected up to seventy years after his death).

Schimmel, Annemarie. *And Muhammad Is His Messenger.* Chapel Hill: University of North Carolina Press, 1985.

————. *As Through a Veil: Mystical Poetry in Islam.* New York: Columbia University Press, 1982.

————. *Mystical Dimensions of Islam.* Chapel Hill: University of North Carolina Press, 1975.

Stoddart, W. *Sufism: The Mystical Doctrines and Methods of Islam.* Wellingsborough, U. K.: Thorsons, 1976.

Thackston, W. M., Jr., translator. *Signs of the Unseen: The Discourses of Rumi.* Putney, Vt.: Threshold, 1994. Another translation of Rumi's *Fīhi Mā Fīhi.*

Valiuddin, Mir. *The Quranic Sufism.* Delhi: Motilal Banarsidass, 1977.

Rumi Translations on the Internet

Gamard, Ibrahim, translator. Dāru 'l-Masnavī website: containing translations of selections from the *Mathnawi* (and some from the *Dīvān*) with commentary, and transliterations of the Persian text, at http://www.dar-al-masnavi.org/

"Sunlight," a Listserv group of daily selections from translations and versions of Rumi's poetry, at http://www.yahoogroups.com/

Index of Passages in Rumi's Works ☐

Acknowledgments □

First, I wish to acknowledge the British scholar Reynold A. Nicholson (1868–1945) for his magnificent full translation and commentary on Rumi's *Mathnawi*, which has been my guide to understanding this masterpiece of Islamic mysticism since 1975. I also wish to express appreciation for the valuable references to the Prophet Muhammad in Rumi's *Dīvān*, which were compiled by the German scholar Annemarie Schimmel (1923–2003) in several books, as well as by her student Dr. John Renard. I wish to express gratitude to Dr. Ravan Farhadi, the Afghan scholar with whom I have been collaborating since 1985, who has provided invaluable assistance in my efforts to translate Rumi from Persian. And finally, I would like to acknowledge Maura Shaw, my first editor at SkyLight Paths Publishing, for discovering my Rumi website (www.dar-al-masnavi.org), appreciating its Islamic orientation, and proposing that I write a book on this very subject.

About SKYLIGHT PATHS Publishing

SkyLight Paths Publishing is creating a place where people of different spiritual traditions come together for challenge and inspiration, a place where we can help each other understand the mystery that lies at the heart of our existence.

Through spirituality, our religious beliefs are increasingly becoming a part of our lives—rather than *apart* from our lives. While many of us may be more interested than ever in spiritual growth, we may be less firmly planted in traditional religion. Yet, we do want to deepen our relationship to the sacred, to learn from our own as well as from other faith traditions, and to practice in new ways.

SkyLight Paths sees both believers and seekers as a community that increasingly transcends traditional boundaries of religion and denomination—people wanting to learn from each other, *walking together, finding the way.*

We at SkyLight Paths take great care to produce beautiful books that present meaningful spiritual content in a form that reflects the art of making high quality books. Therefore, we want to acknowledge those who contributed to the production of this book.

PRODUCTION
Tim Holtz & Bridgett Taylor

EDITORIAL
Maura D. Shaw & Emily Wichland

COVER DESIGN
Walter C. Bumford III, Stockton, Massachusetts

TEXT DESIGN
Chelsea Cloeter, River Forest, Illinois

PRINTING & BINDING
Versa Press, East Peoria, Illinois

Other Interesting Books—Spirituality

Lighting the Lamp of Wisdom: *A Week Inside a Yoga Ashram*
by *John Ittner*; Foreword by *Dr. David Frawley*

This insider's guide to Hindu spiritual life takes you into a typical week of retreat inside a yoga ashram to demystify the experience and show you what to expect from your own visit. Includes a discussion of worship services, meditation and yoga classes, chanting and music, work practice, and more.

6 x 9, 192 pp, b/w photographs, Quality PB, ISBN 1-893361-52-7 **$15.95**;
HC, ISBN 1-893361-37-3 **$24.95**

Waking Up: *A Week Inside a Zen Monastery*
by *Jack Maguire*; Foreword by *John Daido Loori, Roshi*

An essential guide to what it's like to spend a week inside a Zen Buddhist monastery.

6 x 9, 224 pp, b/w photographs, Quality PB, ISBN 1-893361-55-1 **$16.95**;
HC, ISBN 1-893361-13-6 **$21.95**

Making a Heart for God: *A Week Inside a Catholic Monastery*
by *Dianne Aprile*; Foreword by *Brother Patrick Hart, OCSO*

This essential guide to experiencing life in a Catholic monastery takes you to the Abbey of Gethsemani—the Trappist monastery in Kentucky that was home to author Thomas Merton—to explore the details. "More balanced and informative than the popular *The Cloister Walk* by Kathleen Norris." —*Choice: Current Reviews for Academic Libraries*

6 x 9, 224 pp, b/w photographs, Quality PB, ISBN 1-893361-49-7 **$16.95**;
HC, ISBN 1-893361-14-4 **$21.95**

Come and Sit: *A Week Inside Meditation Centers*
by *Marcia Z. Nelson*; Foreword by *Wayne Teasdale*

The insider's guide to meditation in a variety of different spiritual traditions. Traveling through Buddhist, Hindu, Christian, Jewish, and Sufi traditions, this essential guide takes you to different meditation centers to meet the teachers and students and learn about the practices, demystifying the meditation experience.

6 x 9, 224 pp, b/w photographs, Quality PB, ISBN 1-893361-35-7 **$16.95**

Or phone, fax, mail or e-mail to: SKYLIGHT PATHS Publishing
Sunset Farm Offices, Route 4 • P.O. Box 237 • Woodstock, Vermont 05091
Tel: (802) 457-4000 • Fax: (802) 457-4004 • www.skylightpaths.com
Credit card orders: (800) 962-4544 (8:30AM–5:30PM ET Monday–Friday)
Generous discounts on quantity orders. SATISFACTION GUARANTEED. Prices subject to change.

Spiritual Biography

The Life of Evelyn Underhill
An Intimate Portrait of the Groundbreaking Author of Mysticism
by *Margaret Cropper*; Foreword by *Dana Greene*

Evelyn Underhill was a passionate writer and teacher who wrote elegantly on mysticism, worship, and devotional life. This is the story of how she made her way toward spiritual maturity, from her early days of agnosticism to the years when her influence was felt throughout the world. 6 x 9, 288 pp, 5 b/w photos, Quality PB, ISBN 1-893361-70-5 **$18.95**

Zen Effects: *The Life of Alan Watts*
by *Monica Furlong*

The first and only full-length biography of one of the most charismatic spiritual leaders of the twentieth century—now back in print!

Through his widely popular books and lectures, Alan Watts (1915–1973) did more to introduce Eastern philosophy and religion to Western minds than any figure before or since. Here is the only biography of this charismatic figure, who served as Zen teacher, Anglican priest, lecturer, academic, entertainer, a leader of the San Francisco renaissance, and author of more than 30 books, including *The Way of Zen, Psychotherapy East and West* and *The Spirit of Zen.*
6 x 9, 264 pp, Quality PB, ISBN 1-893361-32-2 **$16.95**

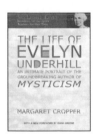 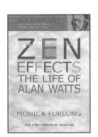  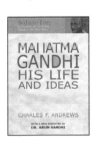

Simone Weil: A Modern Pilgrimage
by *Robert Coles*

The extraordinary life of the spiritual philosopher who's been called both saint and madwoman.

The French writer and philosopher Simone Weil (1906–1943) devoted her life to a search for God—while avoiding membership in organized religion. Robert Coles' intriguing study of Weil details her short, eventful life, and is an insightful portrait of the beloved and controversial thinker whose life and writings influenced many (from T. S. Eliot to Adrienne Rich to Albert Camus), and continue to inspire seekers everywhere. 6 x 9, 208 pp, Quality PB, ISBN 1-893361-34-9 **$16.95**

Mahatma Gandhi: *His Life and Ideas*
by *Charles F. Andrews*; Foreword by *Dr. Arun Gandhi*

An intimate biography of one of the greatest social and religious reformers of the modern world.

Examines from a contemporary Christian activist's point of view the religious ideas and political dynamics that influenced the birth of the peaceful resistance movement, the primary tool that Gandhi and the people of his homeland would use to gain India its freedom from British rule. An ideal introduction to the life and life's work of this great spiritual leader.
6 x 9, 336 pp, 5 b/w photos, Quality PB, ISBN 1-893361-89-6 **$18.95**

Spiritual Practice

Women Pray
Voices through the Ages, from Many Faiths, Cultures, and Traditions
Edited and with introductions by *Monica Furlong*

Many ways—new and old—to communicate with the Divine.

This beautiful gift book celebrates the rich variety of ways women around the world have called out to the Divine—with words of joy, praise, gratitude, wonder, petition, longing, and even anger—from the ancient world up to our own time. Prayers from women of nearly every religious or spiritual background give us an eloquent expression of what it means to communicate with God. 5 x7¼, 256 pp, Deluxe HC with ribbon marker, ISBN 1-893361-25-X **$19.95**

Praying with Our Hands: *Twenty-One Practices of Embodied Prayer from the World's Spiritual Traditions*
by *Jon M. Sweeney*; Photographs by *Jennifer J. Wilson*;
Foreword by *Mother Tessa Bielecki*; Afterword by *Taitetsu Unno, Ph.D.*

A spiritual guidebook for bringing prayer into our bodies.

This inspiring book of reflections and accompanying photographs shows us twenty-one simple ways of using our hands to speak to God, to enrich our devotion and ritual. All express the various approaches of the world's religious traditions to bringing the body into worship. Spiritual traditions represented include Anglican, Sufi, Zen, Roman Catholic, Yoga, Shaker, Hindu, Jewish, Pentecostal, Eastern Orthodox, and many others.
8 x 8, 96 pp, 22 duotone photographs, Quality PB, ISBN 1-893361-16-0 **$16.95**

   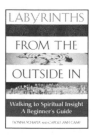

The Sacred Art of Listening
Forty Reflections for Cultivating a Spiritual Practice
by *Kay Lindahl*; Illustrations by *Amy Schnapper*

More than ever before, we need to embrace the skills and practice of listening. You will learn to: Speak clearly from your heart • Communicate with courage and compassion • Heighten your awareness for deep listening • Enhance your ability to listen to people with different belief systems. 8 x 8, 160 pp, Illus., Quality PB, ISBN 1-893361-44-6 **$16.99**

Labyrinths from the Outside In
Walking to Spiritual Insight—a Beginner's Guide
by *Donna Schaper* and *Carole Ann Camp*

The user-friendly, interfaith guide to making and using labyrinths—for meditation, prayer, and celebration.

Labyrinth walking is a spiritual exercise *anyone* can do. This accessible guide unlocks the mysteries of the labyrinth for all of us, providing ideas for using the labyrinth walk for prayer, meditation, and celebrations to mark the most important moments in life. Includes instructions for making a labyrinth of your own and finding one in your area.
6 x 9, 208 pp, b/w illus. and photographs, Quality PB, ISBN 1-893361-18-7 **$16.95**

Spiritual Perspectives

Explores how spiritual beliefs can inform our opinions and transform our actions in areas of social justice and societal change. Tackling the most important—and most divisive—issues of our day, this series provides easy-to-understand introductions to contemporary issues. Readers aren't told what to think; rather, they're given information—*spiritual* perspectives—in order to reach their own conclusions.

Spiritual Perspectives on America's Role as Superpower
by *the Editors at SkyLight Paths*
Are we the world's good neighbor or a global bully?
Explores broader issues surrounding the use of American power around the world, including in Iraq and the Middle East. From a spiritual perspective, what are America's responsibilities as the only remaining superpower? Contributors:

Dr. Beatrice Bruteau • Rev. Dr. Joan Brown Campbell • Tony Campolo • Rev. Forrest Church • Lama Surya Das • Matthew Fox • Kabir Helminski • Thich Nhat Hanh • Eboo Patel • Abbot M. Basil Pennington, ocso • Dennis Prager • Rosemary Radford Ruether • Wayne Teasdale • Rev. William McD. Tully • Rabbi Arthur Waskow • John Wilson
5½ x 8½, 256 pp, Quality PB, ISBN 1-893361-81-0 **$16.95**

 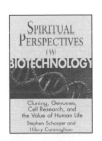 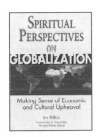

Spiritual Perspectives on Biotechnology
Cloning, Genomes, Cell Research, and the Value of Human Life
by *Stephen Scharper* and *Hilary Cunningham*
A balanced introduction to the issues of biotechnology.
From genetically modified foods through cloning of animals and life forms, explains in clear and nonjudgmental language the beliefs that motivate religious leaders, activists, theologians, academics, and others involved on all sides of biotechnology issues. Many different perspectives are included—representing all of the world's largest faith traditions and many other spiritual persuasions.
5½ x 8½, 235 pp, Quality PB, ISBN 1-893361-58-6 **$16.99**

Spiritual Perspectives on Globalization
Making Sense of Economic and Cultural Upheaval
by *Ira Rifkin*; Foreword by *Dr. David Little, Harvard Divinity School*
What is globalization? What are spiritually-minded people saying and doing about it?
This lucid introduction surveys the religious landscape, explaining in clear and nonjudgmental language the beliefs that motivate spiritual leaders, activists, theologians, academics, and others involved on all sides of the issue.
5½ x 8½, 224 pp, Quality PB, ISBN 1-893361-57-8 **$16.95**

SkyLight Illuminations Series
Andrew Harvey, series editor

Offers today's spiritual seeker an enjoyable entry into the great classic texts of the world's spiritual traditions. Each classic is presented in an accessible translation, with facing pages of guided commentary from experts, giving you the keys you need to understand the history, context, and meaning of the text. This series enables readers of all backgrounds to experience and understand classic spiritual texts directly, and to make them a part of their lives. Andrew Harvey writes the foreword to each volume, an insightful, personal introduction to each classic.

Bhagavad Gita: *Annotated & Explained*
Translation by *Shri Purohit Swami*; Annotation by *Kendra Crossen Burroughs*
"The very best Gita for first-time readers." —Ken Wilber
Millions of people turn daily to India's most beloved holy book, whose universal appeal has made it popular with non-Hindus and Hindus alike. This edition introduces you to the characters; explains references and philosophical terms; shares the interpretations of famous spiritual leaders and scholars; and more. 5½ x 8½, 192 pp, Quality PB, ISBN 1-893361-28-4 **$16.95**

  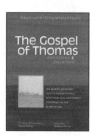

The Way of a Pilgrim: *Annotated & Explained*
Translation and annotation by *Gleb Pokrovsky*
The classic of Russian spirituality—now with facing-page commentary that illuminates and explains the text for you.
This delightful account is the story of one man who sets out to learn the prayer of the heart—also known as the "Jesus prayer"—and how the practice transforms his existence. This edition guides you through an abridged version of the text with facing-page annotations explaining the names, terms and references. 5½ x 8½, 160 pp, Quality PB, ISBN 1-893361-31-4 **$14.95**

The Gospel of Thomas: *Annotated & Explained*
Translation and annotation by *Stevan Davies*
The recently discovered mystical sayings of Jesus—now with facing-page commentary that illuminates and explains the text for you.
Discovered in 1945, this collection of aphoristic sayings sheds new light on the origins of Christianity and the intriguing figure of Jesus, portraying the Kingdom of God as a present fact about the world, rather than a future promise or future threat. This edition guides you through the text with annotations that focus on the meaning of the sayings, ideal for readers with no previous background in Christian history or thought.
5½ x 8½, 192 pp, Quality PB, ISBN 1-893361-45-4 **$16.95**

SkyLight Illuminations Series
Andrew Harvey, series editor

Zohar: *Annotated & Explained*
Translation and annotation by *Daniel C. Matt*

The cornerstone text of Kabbalah.

The best-selling author of *The Essential Kabbalah* brings together in one place the most important teachings of the *Zohar*, the canonical text of Jewish mystical tradition. Guides you step by step through the midrash, mystical fantasy and Hebrew scripture that make up the *Zohar*, explaining the inner meanings in facing-page commentary. Ideal for readers without any prior knowledge of Jewish mysticism.

5½ x 8½, 176 pp, Quality PB, ISBN 1-893361-51-9 **$15.99**

Selections from the Gospel of Sri Ramakrishna
Annotated & Explained
Translation by *Swami Nikhilananda*; Annotation by *Kendra Crossen Burroughs*

The words of India's greatest example of God-consciousness and mystical ecstasy in recent history.

Introduces the fascinating world of the Indian mystic and the universal appeal of his message that has inspired millions of devotees for more than a century. Selections from the original text and insightful yet unobtrusive commentary highlight the most important and inspirational teachings. Ideal for readers without any prior knowledge of Hinduism.

5½ x 8½, 240 pp, b/w photographs, Quality PB, ISBN 1-893361-46-2 **$16.95**

 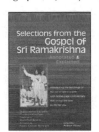  

Dhammapada: *Annotated & Explained*
Translation by *Max Müller* and revised by *Jack Maguire*; Annotation by *Jack Maguire*

The classic of Buddhist spiritual practice.

The Dhammapada—words spoken by the Buddha himself over 2,500 years ago—is notoriously difficult to understand for the first-time reader. Now you can experience it with understanding even if you have no previous knowledge of Buddhism. Enlightening facing-page commentary explains all the names, terms, and references, giving you deeper insight into the text.

5½ x 8½, 160 pp, Quality PB, ISBN 1-893361-42-X **$14.95**

Hasidic Tales: *Annotated & Explained*
Translation and annotation by *Rabbi Rami Shapiro*

The legendary tales of the impassioned Hasidic rabbis.

The allegorical quality of Hasidic tales can be perplexing. Here, they are presented as stories rather than parables, making them accessible and meaningful. Each demonstrates the spiritual power of unabashed joy, offers lessons for leading a holy life, and reminds us that the Divine can be found in the everyday. Annotations explain theological concepts, introduce major characters, and clarify references unfamiliar to most readers.

5½ x 8½, 240 pp, Quality PB, ISBN 1-893361-86-1 **$16.95**

Reli[...]nce

How to Be a Perfect Stranger, 3rd Edition
The Essential Religious Etiquette Handbook
Edited by *Stuart M. Matlins* and *Arthur J. Magida*

The indispensable guidebook to help the well-meaning guest when visiting other people's religious ceremonies.

A straightforward guide to the rituals and celebrations of the major religions and denominations in the United States and Canada from the perspective of an interested guest of any other faith, based on information obtained from authorities of each religion. Belongs in every living room, library, and office.

COVERS:

African American Methodist Churches • Assemblies of God • Baha'i • Baptist • Buddhist • Christian Church (Disciples of Christ) • Christian Science (Church of Christ, Scientist) • Churches of Christ • Episcopalian and Anglican • Hindu • Islam • Jehovah's Witnesses • Jewish • Lutheran • Mennonite/Amish • Methodist • Mormon (Church of Jesus Christ of Latter-day Saints) • Native American/First Nations • Orthodox Churches • Pentecostal Church of God • Presbyterian • Quaker (Religious Society of Friends) • Reformed Church in America/Canada • Roman Catholic • Seventh-day Adventist • Sikh • Unitarian Universalist • United Church of Canada • United Church of Christ

6 x 9, 432 pp, Quality PB, ISBN 1-893361-67-5 **$19.95**

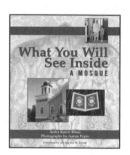

What You Will See Inside A Mosque
by *Aisha Karen Kahn*; Photographs by *Aaron Pepis*

A colorful, fun-to-read introduction that explains the ways and whys of Muslim faith and worship.

Visual and informative, featuring full-page pictures and concise descriptions of what is happening, the objects used, the spiritual leaders and laypeople who have specific roles, and the spiritual intent of the believers.

Ideal for children as well as teachers, partents, librarians, clergy, and lay leaders who want to demystify the celebrations and ceremonies of Islam throughout the year, as well as encourage understanding and tolerance among different faith traditions.

8½ x 10½, 32 pp, Full-color photographs, Hardcover, ISBN 1-893361-60-8 **$16.95**